So You Want to be a Landlord?

So You Want to be a Landlord?

A Practical and Humorous How-to Book for the Rental Owner

Patricia Hartmann

iUniverse, Inc.

New York   Lincoln   Shanghai

So You Want to be a Landlord?
A Practical and Humorous How-to Book for the Rental Owner

iUniverse, Inc.

For information address:
iUniverse, Inc.
2021 Pine Lake Road, Suite 100
Lincoln, NE 68512
www.iuniverse.com

ISBN: 0-595-31214-4

Printed in the United States of America

Contents

Forword

I never planned on being a landlord. Blame it on love.

When I first met my husband, he was already heavily invested in real estate. I didn't give it much thought until after we were married. In this **after** part, I began to realize just how much time rentals took. This was…after my husband fielded the late night phone calls for plumbing emergencies…after the Saturdays spent cleaning out rentals…. after seeing my husband slaving over a tumbling pile of bills at night.

I realized that if we were to ever have any quality time together (time doing something more uplifting than cleaning out calcified toilet bowls), I'd better shoulder a bit of the load.

We both had full time jobs. My husband was a school principal. I was a high school English teacher. We had a his/mine/and ours family of eight children. We lived in a 140-year-old farmhouse. We ran a swim school during the summer. We planted Christmas trees on our property and sold them during Christmas break. We had busy lives. I knew nothing about being a landlord. But I could learn.

Motivated by the image of time with my honey, I plunged into the nitty gritty of being a landlord. I took phone calls, interviewed prospective tenants, painted walls, hauled away trash. I hired plumbers, wrote checks, deposited rents. I made mistakes. Lots of mistakes. I tried to find the balance between caring about people and running a business.

My husband and I bought more rental property. I retired from teaching and took on even more of the rental business. Before I knew it…I was a landlord. Twenty-five years later, I'm still at it.

Everyone takes a different path to becoming a landlord. This was mine.

I hope your time as a landlord is a interesting a ride as mine has been.

Pat Hartmann

Introduction

So, you want to be a landlord? You are considering renting out the cute little studio over the garage, buying a house that includes a granny flat, or pulling your sinking portfolio out of the stock market to invest in real estate. This is the book for you. Included in these pages are the nuts and bolts of landlording from plumbing to evictions. This book provides all the information, forms, cautionary tales, legalities, and sage advice you will need to take on the mantle of "The Landlord." You see, being a landlord is not as easy as it first seems. Why should you make your own costly landlording mistakes when you can learn from mine?

My husband and I have been landlords for over 20 years. Real estate is our side business. Our properties include apartments, rental houses and the occasional triplex. Most of them are in small to medium priced, nice family-oriented communities. We are not big-time corporation absentee landlords. We are the small-time hands-on rental owner. While we haven't seen it all, we've seen enough.

Being a landlord isn't all it's cracked up to be. In fact, many landlords end up feeling a bit cracked up themselves. Renting a house or an apartment is supposed to be a business agreement—all neatly spelled out on paper and signed by both parties. But the party is most likely to be in your rental property and the damages are on you.

Let me say up front that there are a lot of good tenants out there. They know who they are. They pay the rent on time each month. They fix up the yard, have your carpets cleaned, mow the grass, wash the windows, happily abide by the terms of the rental agreement and spend money out of their own pocket for minor repairs. They are a good neighbor and leave the rental in better shape than you found it. They take pride in their home, know how to manage their money and they are probably saving up right now to buy their own house. My hat is off to them. They make it possible to keep your sanity in this business. If all tenants were like them, I wouldn't need to write this book. It would be a snap to be a landlord—just a handshake…a smile…collect the rent…watch your investment grow.

But unfortunately, all tenants aren't so responsible. It only takes a few bad apples to spoil the barrel. And they can bring the landlord a barrelful of trouble. It is these challenging tenants and their stories that flesh out this book. They provide the cautionary tales of what to do when the unthinkable happens, or better yet how to keep it from happening in the first place. People are full of surprises. Some tenants are especially prone to put themselves and their needs first. Today's landlord is certain to face his share of tangles with tenants. There is sure to be unpaid rent, uninvited guests, upset neighbors and a few unexpected legal challenges thrown in.

The tenant's problems can very quickly become your problems. A late alimony check, job change, illness, or car breakdown can be an excuse to not pay the rent. You are the landlord. Since you are rich, you can always wait to be paid until your tenant meets his other more pressing obligations like new car payments, vacation trips, or sometimes even drugs and alcohol. Whether or not the rent comes in on time, as the landlord, you are expected to not only provide their housing and utilities but to also be their banker, problem solver, counselor, repairman, and mediator of feuds between tenants. You will be on call 24/7. When things go wrong, no matter how nice you think you are, you will always be the bad guy, attempting to impose the rules of the rental agreement.

Still with me? You really want to be a landlord? Then this book is for you—intrepid warrior that you are. Each chapter starts with a pull out from the rental agreement that covers the chapter topic. The anecdotes are intended to give an insight as to the endless possibilities of tenant behavior from making excuses to sneaking in pets. The "Getting it Right" section at the end of each chapter is a lifeline revealing the pitfalls, legalities, and some tactics that work in each area of the landlord/tenant relationship. A checklist is provided for each chapter to give you a quick and easy way to see if that area is covered for your rental. At the end of the book is a reproducible selection of the many forms you will need as a landlord—ranging from the rental application to the disposition of any sundry items left behind.

You are the landlord. Good luck and fasten your seat belt. Life is just about to get a whole lot more exciting.

Chapter 1

Buying the Rental Property

*The Owner rents to the Tenant and the Tenant rents from the Owner, for residential use only, the premises known as*_____

Street Address

_____   _____.*

State   Zip Code

*This is a portion of the Rental Agreement.

To Buy or not to Buy…That is the Question

Why would you want to invest in rental property? Why not? Your life is pretty dull right now…and a few tenants are sure to liven things up a bit. Oh, you're not bored? Well then maybe you are just a shrewd investor. Real estate is one of the most solid investments you can make. When a rental unit is located on that piece of real estate, you not only gain the appreciation of the property, but you are collecting rent as well. If you can get in with a low down payment, your rental can more than pay for itself. You are acquiring property and making a profit as well.

Rentals are a much more secure investment than a volatile stock market. One bullish trader snidely remarked that no stock or bond had ever called him up in the middle of the night to complain about a leaking toilet. My response is, *"Maybe so, but at the end of the unexpected stock market dive, when you are left with a worthless piece of paper, at least I'll still have the toilet."*

What to Look For

Before you can get into the swing of being a landlord, you first have to have some land to lord it over. Unless you have inherited a rental unit, this means buying a rental property. What are you looking for?

Profit

First of all, it is desirable to actually make a profit. This means that you have to do the math to decide if the cost of the rental unit you are considering can be covered by a realistic rent after subtracting the expenses like mortgage payments, fixing up the rental, utilities, insurance, taxes, upkeep, and repairs. You will also want to figure in the probable appreciation of the property. Even if the rental is an alligator, eating all of your profits on paper, the property is likely to go up in value.

Number of Units

Do you want a single unit like a house, or multiple units like an apartment building? In general, the more units located on a given property the bigger your cash return will be. Of course more units mean more tenants, which mean more headaches.

Location

Location is also a key consideration. Is the proposed rental located in a good neighborhood or a high crime area? What types of tenants would want to live there? What are rentals going for in this area? How close is it to your home? Will it be easy to take care of or will the distance make it difficult to manage?

Condition

Condition is also important. What kind of shape is the house or apartment complex in? Cosmetic improvements like paint and carpeting are easy fixes. But if the unit needs a new roof, has old plumbing and wiring, or needs a total makeover, your outlay before renting will be much higher. If possible, always buy a creampuff. If you choose to go with a fixer-upper make a calculated guess as to the cost of repairs and then double it. It will always cost twice as much as you'd imagine to get a place ready to rent.

Professional Help

Along the way you will probably need the services of a real-estate agent to show you the properties available and an escrow agent to get the deal down legally on paper. Maybe you will need to secure a loan. Once you decide you are interested in a possible rental, the bidding begins. If you are lucky, you can close the deal on your dream rental.

When the Fat Lady Sings:
An Escrow is not Over 'til it's Over

Not all escrows go as smoothly as you might like. We began an escrow with an elderly woman, Mrs. Wiley, who wanted to sell her home to move out of state and live with her daughter. On our first trip to the escrow office, Mrs. Wiley got cold feet. She wasn't sure she wanted to sell after all. We drove her back home and encouraged her to do what she felt comfortable with. A few days later she called. The deal was on. Another trip to the escrow office. This time she felt dizzy. By the third trip, our escrow check was getting outdated. But this time she signed on the dotted line and seemed content with the change in her life.

Mrs. Wiley had wanted to leave some items behind, so we paid her a sizeable sum on the side for the tools and fishing gear that had belonged to her late husband. After she moved out and we took possession, we looked for the tools and the fishing gear that we had purchased from her. They were gone. A little investigation revealed that she had sold the tools twice, the second time to the neighbor across the fence. We had to pay the neighbor his price to get our tools back again. The fishing gear never did turn up. I envisioned Mrs. Wiley happily fishing off the dock at her new home; smug in the little scam she had pulled off.

About a year later Mrs. Wiley called. She wanted to buy her old home back at the old selling price even though we had by now invested plenty in repairs and had it rented. This time I wasn't biting.

As they say, *it's not over until the fat lady sings*—or when buying property, until the previous owner signs. The escrow office can be the place for many a change of heart. Once we began a deal to buy an apartment house from an out-of-town relative for whom we'd been managing it over the years. After the papers were drawn up, he changed his mind. Several years later he again wanted us to buy it, of course at a higher price by now. This time, the papers actually got signed. A few nights later he called up wanting to back out of the deal. He offered a few thousand dollars for us to give back the property. A deal is a deal, so this time we declined.

I've also been in a few bidding wars. Especially in times of inflation, housing prices can shoot up overnight. Once we were bidding on a triplex. Over the course of a week, a competitor bested our every bid. After dropping out of the bidding, we found that we had lost out to one of our neighbors who had been bidding against us. Our ignorance of each other's identity had driven the price up considerably.

Don't get too attached to a property that you are bidding on. Life has a way of evening the playing field. We once put in a bid on a cute little seaside property. Our bid was used to jack up the offer of another buyer in an unethical manner. We felt sort of sad to lose out due to some underhanded tactics by the agent. For years we envied the new owner. Twenty years later, a massive landslide hit the seaside community, completely burying the little beach house. Overnight it was reduced to rubble under a ton of mud. My envy was reduced to relief.

Getting It Right

Getting the Biggest Bang for your Buck

Two monetary factors to consider before buying a rental property are the number of units on the property and leverage.

In general, the more units you have on a property, the higher the percentage of return you can expect per unit. For example, a ten-unit apartment building will bring in more than a triplex, a triplex more than a duplex and a duplex more than a single-family house on the same piece of land. The downside is that the more units you have, the more tenants you will need to deal with. You also have to buy what you can afford.

Leverage is another factor in buying a rental investment. In inflationary times, the smaller the amount of money you put down on a rental, the greater leverage you have. For example, if you have $10,000 invested in a down payment on a $200,000 house, and the house goes up $10,000 in value, theoretically you have made a 100% return on your investment. However, if you had paid the full $200,000 in cash for the same house and the house went up the same $10,000, you have made only a 5% return on you investment. Because of the leverage factor, the smaller down payment you make, the larger your investment return. Your mortgage payments however will be higher with a lesser down payment.

A good deal in real estate is when you can make an income of 1% of the value of the property each month. This would be about a 10% return per year after expenses. For a $300,000 house, this would mean a rent of almost $3000 per month. You are unlikely to be able to charge that much. But let's say you charge $1500 per month for about a 5% return per year. This doesn't sound too good until you figure in the appreciation. Most property is appreciating at about 10% per year. This gives you a total profit of 15% on your investment per year. How does that sound?!

Appreciation

No, I'm not talking about applause here. If you want cheering—become an actor. If you want a good sound investment, consider real estate. If the price of houses and other rental units are high in your area, the going rate of rent may not keep up with the cost of the investment. In some cases your rental might actually be an alligator as far as income goes, taking you into the swampy hole each month with a negative cash flow. If this is the case, you will have to decide if the appreciation factor is worth it. In a bullish market with strong inflation, the inflationary factor alone in the value of your rental property might be 10 percent. Your $200,000 investment might be worth $300,000 in five years. In any case, your rental is in a tax-sheltered investment.

The Tax Sale

One cut-rate way to buy a rental is through a tax sale. Houses repossessed for back taxes can often be bought for far less than the going rate. Cultivate a good relationship with your banker, as the deal is often done on a cash-only basis. Be sure to check out any other existing liens on the property before committing. A lien is a monetary claim on the property as security for a debt. We once made the mistake of not checking this out, and found an additional second mortgage lien of $20,000 after we had bought the house. We were now responsible for this amount—a fact that made a great deal, only an OK deal.

Buy a Creampuff or Enroll in Home Repair CPR

When sizing up a rental unit, the easiest route is to buy a creampuff—a house or apartment that is in excellent ready-to-move-in shape. Now that you've toyed with this pipe dream, wake up and smell the wet plaster. The reality is that most rental property in an affordable price range needs some work or a lot of work to make it rentable. If it is in poor shape, hopefully its woeful condition will be reflected in a lower price, as it always costs more for repairs that you imagine. When in doubt, get a few estimates on the repairs needed before you buy. A true fixer-upper usually means that you need to up your skills in painting, plumbing and patching, or be willing to pay to hire someone with these skills. Decide if you want to tackle major repairs or if you want to pay more for a rental already in good condition.

After sizing up one of our best rental buys, an older house in need of lots of TLC, one carpenter told us that we'd best start with a match. After hiring a more optimistic carpenter, it took us several years until the rent paid for the needed repairs, but now this house is a good moneymaker for us.

You will need to look at a potential rental with an eye to the possibilities. Painting, replacing carpeting and mowing the lawn are easy fixes. A total bath or kitchen remodel or putting on a new roof can be an expensive proposition.

Remember that as the landlord you have a responsibility to provide a clean and safe housing unit. You can not rent a place with broken windows, no screens, holes in the walls, dripping faucets, sagging floors, non-functioning locks, or a leaking roof. One lawsuit over an unfenced pool, a fall through an unsafe railing or a real or imagined illness due to a faulty heater can dampen any dreams of happily ever after.

Find a good Real Estate Agent

If you are in the market to buy some rental property, a good real estate agent is key. Find one who has actually looked at the properties he is listing. This may sound a bit skeptical, but we have dealt with a fair share of agents who are doing their first walk-through of a property with you. This means that this agent will not know the answers to your most basic questions. A real estate agent is taking a pretty good chunk of money for "helping" you find a place, so he should at least do his homework. I expect a good agent to ask me questions about what type of place I'm looking for, the price range I want, the type of neighborhood, and the kind of escrow I want. I expect him to have asked the seller lots of questions as well.

I also expect the real estate agent to be able to answer most of my questions about the house. If he doesn't really know anything about the house, and just responds with "Well, I'll have to ask," to your most basic questions, why do you need him? A poor agent can actually bungle the deal for you. He can use your bid to get another bidder to come in higher. He can move slowly in presenting your bid and cause you to miss the deal.

A friend who was new to town was looking at a house in our neighborhood. He asked us to look at it with him as his real estate agent was away on a vacation. We looked at the place, but knew of a better house for his needs just across town. Real estate was selling quickly in this area. We didn't want him to miss out on the perfect house for him. Since his agent was on vacation, we called the owner and arranged a walk-through. We did the deal with a few phone calls. Our friend bought the wonderful house, which he loved. His real estate agent returned a few weeks later to collect his commission for doing nothing.

A good real estate agent should know some comparisons (comps) for the neighborhood. That is he should have found out what similar houses have sold for in the area. This will give you an idea if the house is priced too high or is at an attractive price. If you are looking at an apartment complex, he should know what rents are being charged for similar units in the area.

Splitting the Commission

Today it is getting more common to have to deal with two real estate agents. One representing the seller and one representing you, as the buyer. If you are dealing with two agents they will have to split the 6% commission as well as give fees to their respective offices. This greatly lowers their incentive to give you good service or a good deal. So here is a little trick of the trade. What you want is to deal directly with the agent who is representing the seller. *"What?"* I hear you asking.

Let me explain. Let's say you go to your realtor friend, Joe Schmo and say, *"Hey Joe, I trust you as an agent. Can you find a rental house for me?"* If Joe doesn't have what you want in his own listings, he then goes to the multiple listings. Right away you are dealing with that second agent.

But let's say you are smart enough to check the listings in the paper yourself. You see several likely prospects listed by "Home Sweet Home Reality." If you call up this office directly to look at the houses of interest, you're dealing with the seller's agent. Let's say the seller is asking $400,000 for the house you want. His agent, who is likely drawing an average 6 % commission, will get $24,000 from the deal. But you are only willing to pay $350,000 for the house. Now he will get only $21,000, but that's still a good amount of money. And if he doesn't sell the house he gets nothing. If Joe Schmo had found the same house for you, which is not his listing, he and the "Home Sweet Home" realtor would have to split the commission and pay fees to two offices. Now the take for each realtor is down to about $10,500. You can see why the listing realtor would much rather deal with you directly. Even if he advises his seller to take a more realistic lower price, he wins. And so do you.

The listing agent is employed by the seller and therefore has a fiduciary responsibility to get the best possible price for his client; however the seller may have an unrealistic price or selling time line. The listing agent wants to make the deal for the sake of his client as well as himself.

Questions to Ask

When you are looking at potential rental properties, it pays to know the right questions to ask. You want to find out as much as possible about the condition of the unit and what repairs have and have not been done lately. How old is the roof? Most roofs are good for about 20 years. Is the house on sewer or septic? If it is on septic, when have the tanks been pumped last. (A septic tank that has not been pumped for 3+ years is likely to have developed leech line problems.) How old is the wiring? How up to date is the electrical panel? Since most tenants will have more than one computer, a stereo system, a microwave, several TV's, and other electrically driven gadgets, older electrical systems might be inadequate. Does the yard have a sprinkling system? Does it work? Are any appliances like a stove or built in microwave being left? How old is the stove? The microwave? Is it in good working order? How old are the carpets, the sinks, the toilets? Any problems with the house? Flooding, weeping walls, termite damage, broken fixtures? While the seller is required by law to fully disclose any such problems, it doesn't always happen.

A friend bought a house in good condition. She had not paid much attention to the rubber mat covering the bottom of the sink. After she moved in, she removed the mat and was shocked to discover that the double sink had a huge chunk of enamel missing. The mat had been hiding the rusting damaged portion of the sink that necessitated replacing the double sink and the tile countertop as well.

So don't be timid. Look in the cupboards. Pick up the throw rugs. Turn on the faucets. Switch on the lights. Try out the heater. Looks for signs of leaks like discolored ceilings or walls or bubbling of the walls. I once noticed a sidewall of a downstairs bedroom that had strange bubbling of the new paint. The seller admitted that the wall was located below the graded dirt level and that moisture was coming in from the recent rains. A closer look outside revealed elaborate drainage devices that had been tried unsuccessfully to fix the problem. But dirt three feet high resting against a house wall is a lethal problem.

Do the current owners have pets? What have they done about flea control? Has grain been stored on the property to feed birds or larger animals? Has this caused a rat problem?

If possible, ask the neighbors about the house. Any flooding problems in the area? How is the neighborhood? Any loud parties? Crime problems? How are the local schools? Are rentals allowed in this area? If possible drive by this house several times including on a Saturday night to get a feel for the activity on the street.

Liability Issues

Looking for a rental house is different than looking for a house for your own home. Certain amenities that you might like to have at home might be a liability in a rental. A swimming pool for instance, is an accident waiting to happen. We have a pool at our home, but here I am the one responsible to see that the gates are always latched and it is maintained in good condition. At a rental you are asking for trouble. Who will clean it and maintain the chemical balance? Who will pay for the pool maintenance? What extra liability insurance is needed? Even a pool located next door can affect your liability. What if the common fence is damaged and your tenant's child gets into the neighbor's pool. Who is liable? Even small ponds raise liability issues.

A large shade tree can also be a liability. What if a big branch comes down on the house or worse yet on a tenant? Who will keep the trees pruned and the leaves raked? Who will mow the expansive lawns and pay for the water?

That spiked wrought iron fence out front is nice to look at, but is it safe for a family with small children? Would the railings on the stairway and upstairs landing at the apartment you're considering prevent a small child from falling through? Are they up to code? Keep an eye to safety and ease of maintenance when considering a house as a rental.

Escrow

You've found the house you want, have thoroughly checked it out, and you are ready to buy. You and the seller have agreed on a price and most of the terms. If you are taking out a loan you have had an appraisal done and probably a termite inspection as required by law. Your next stop is the escrow office.

Escrow is where all of the official documents are drawn up. Here buyer and seller come together to spell out the details from the selling price to who will pay for a termite inspection and treatment. These are not details to be scribbled on a piece of paper. They need to be legally drawn up and often registered with the county.

Here you will work out with the seller such issues as who will pay for the tenting or preventative work if termite problems are found. Will the sale have any contingencies such as being contingent on you being able to get a loan for a certain amount at a certain interest rate? Does it hinge on the sale of other property? How long is the escrow period? Will it be a 30-day escrow or one much longer or much shorter? Is the owner carrying back paper on the house? How much is the down payment? Will there be a prepayment penalty if you pay off the loan sooner? What will your move in date be?

The escrow officer is trained to guide you through the process and to make sure that all 7000 documents are signed by both parties at the bottom. (OK, maybe it's only seven documents.)

When you finish escrow, you should have in your hand your Grant Deed, the Loan Documents, the Note (which details all the terms of your agreement), and a Title Insurance Policy (which insures that no liens exist on the property.) That wasn't so bad now was it?

Congratulations! You are a Landlord. Now the fun begins!

Buying the Rental Property Checklist:

❑ Get the biggest bang for your buck.

❑ Consider appreciation and the tax sale.

❑ Buy a cream puff or find good repairmen.

❑ Find a good real estate agent. (The seller's agent is best.)

❑ Ask the right questions.

❑ Agree to terms you can live with.

❑ Complete the escrow.

You are the landlord…Buckle up for a rollicking ride on the rental roller coaster.

*This form is located at the back of this book.

Chapter 2

Advertising and Showing the Rental

Unfurnished Houses for Rent

Smallville. 3+2 w/den, f/p
near downtown,
lots of light .dbl.
grg. mtn. vws. np,ns.
1850/mo + $2800 dep.
555-3647

The Blind Date

Once you have a house or apartment ready to rent, the next step is to find a suitable tenant. This is somewhat like going out on a blind date. You are hopeful, but don't really know what's out there. How can rental and renter meet and begin a blissful relationship? This is where the dating agency comes in. The Want Ads are your ticket to connect the lovelorn tenant with your lovely rental on their first blind date.

When one of our first rental ads came out in the paper, we were shocked to get our first call at 6:30 in the morning. Before the day was out we had received 60 phone calls about our cute little country house. This told us something. First that rentals were in big demand, and secondly—forget about having a life while your ad is running.

If possible try to make time to be by the phone when your ad comes out. Otherwise you will return home to that blinking light on your answering machine which signals that you have 30 calls to return. It can be quite a game of phone tag. For people who watch the want ads, the first day of your ad will be it's hottest phone day. They have been waiting and watching for a decent rental to come vacant and you have it. Like a good man, a good rental is often hard to find.

After the ad comes out, you will be answering the phone a lot. The prospective tenant will want to ask a few questions and you will want to ask a few of your own. This is the first stage of he blind date—the exchange of information. Have a notebook handy and write down the information about each person. Otherwise the callers will all start running together in your head. Write down your impressions about this person and start probing to see if they seem right for your rental. You can ask a series of questions that will help you get a feel for this tenant and his situation.

Who Will Live There?

When interviewing a prospective tenant on the phone, find out who he expects to have living with him. The more people in your rental house, the greater the wear and tear—on the rental and on your nerves. The number of showers, sinkfuls of dirty dishes and flushes per day that your system can tolerate can be computed numerically by using the multiplier of the number of proposed tenants divided by the liquid cubic foot capacity of your septic system. (Just Kidding...) In other words, more is <u>not</u> merrier for your pipes or your septic tank. Are there enough bedrooms to house the ten relatives and their respective boyfriends, girlfriends and children, or will the living room and garage be put into use and sectioned off with hanging sheets and mattresses on the floor?

Beware of the prospective tenant who wants to know how many people he can have in your rental. Some people expect to open their door (in this case the landlord's door) to his many relatives. He may agree to only four people but forgets to mention the unending supply of relatives who, along with their small children and assorted pets, will be visiting on a rotating basis. Your rental can quickly become home to any number of *guests* who are just there until they get established, get a good job, get married or get evicted, whichever comes first.

The young adult who wants two or three roommates to help pay the rent is also a red flag. Your rental is doomed to become a sort of hotel for those who are between classes, jobs and girlfriends. They will come and go at an alarming rate along with all manner of overnight girlfriends, boyfriends, and friends of friends. Parties are inevitable as are broken windows, hearts, and rental agreements.

Other questions to ask in this initial phone conversation are: When do you need a place? Why are you moving? Do you have any pets? Are you familiar with this area?

Getting It Right

Advertising

Finding the best tenant begins with advertising your rental unit. Word of mouth sometime works. If you have a good tenant who is giving you notice, ask him if he knows someone who might be interested in the house or apartment. We have found many good tenants this way and never had to actually advertise.

Putting a "For Rent" sign out front will catch the eye of people driving through the neighborhood who are already familiar with the area and might want to live there. They get a curbside view of your rental and know up front if this might be a place suitable for them. You can only put so much information on the sign however so this means answering a lot of questions when they phone. I hang up a sign and place an ad in the newspaper.

Newspaper advertising is usually your best bet. Placing a classified ad in the "Unfurnished Apartments for Rent" or the "Unfurnished Houses for Rent" section is as easy as a phone call or E-mail and is not too expensive. Often a paper with a larger circulation gives you a better result than relying only on the small town paper. You are charged by the word or line, so keep your ad brief and to the point. You may want to pay extra to put in a few highlights that might attract a tenant such as if your rental has a garage, a yard, or if it is in a good part of town. A detail or two like this also sets your ad apart.

The newspaper will abbreviate commonly used words or phrases to cut the length. For example a three bedroom two bath will be written as a 3+2. A fireplace becomes a fp. You don't need to say house or apartment as it is already listed under that heading. Frame your ad to weed out the tenant you don't want before they call. Be sure to say "No Smoking" (n/s) or "No Pets" (n/p) if this is what you want. By law, you are not allowed to specify "adults only" or "no children" although you can screen for the number of people and ages right for your unit. The law does permit having a senior's only apartment building.

Listing the city or area and whether it is upstairs helps you to screen out the prospective tenant who can't get upstairs or doesn't want your area of town before they call. Include in your ad any extras you provide like a gardener, a garage, or a fenced yard and be sure to put in the rent amount plus security deposit and your phone number. You might want to list the date the rental will be available. If my unit has a special selling point, I try to list it to make the ad stand out. Lots of light, hardwood floors, big trees, fenced back yard are all assets. Saying that your rental is **nice** doesn't really say anything. It is better to say upgraded, newly painted, view of mountains, close to good elementary school, or quiet neighborhood.

A typical ad looks something like this:

Rentals, Houses
3+2 w/den, f/p, new pnt.,
dbl. grg., mtn. vws.,
¼ acre, trsh/wtr., $1800/mo.
+$2300 dep. 555-3647

This translates as a three bedroom two bath house with a den, fireplace, new paint and double garage. It has mountain views on one-fourth of an acre. The landlord pays trash and water and is asking $1800 a month rent with a $2300 security deposit.

Another example:

Rentals, Apartments
Small 2+1 pvt. yd, O.V.,
w/d hook-ups, n/s n/p.
$900/mo.+ dep. 555-9956

This is a small two-bedroom one-bath apartment in the town of Oak View. It has washer/dryer hookups and is a non-smoking, no-pet apartment renting for $900 a month.

Be sure to cancel your ad when your unit is rented, as it will save you from getting a lot of unnecessary phone calls, and paying for an ad you don't need.

Other ways to advertise your rental are to contact a listing agency or a real estate firm in town. Some keep a listing of rentals for their clients.

The Phone Conversation

When a prospective tenant calls, jot down some notes next to his name in a special notebook. Note such things as the number of people in the family, any pets, and the volume of the stereo in the background. If the background noise is loud, this will probably not be a nice, quiet tenant. If a child is screaming, and the tenant says the rental is just for herself and her husband, ask about the youngster. Maybe she is planning on running childcare out of your house. It happens.

I usually say up front that I am looking for a long-term tenant. Some people want a temporary place while they are waiting for a house to be built, to buy a home, or to make a move out of town. For me, a short-term tenancy is not worth the extra work. (See more on this in the Chapter 15 on Clean Up) Ask why he is moving from his present space. This can be telling. If he complains about ill treatment by his present landlord, or seem kind of vague this sends up a red flag. If his last landlord has it in for him, chances are he deserved it. You will be next on his rag-on-the-landlord list— since you are one. If the response to why he is moving is something vague like, *"Oh I'm just looking for a different place,"* be sure to check if he is currently being evicted or has a poor credit history.

Ask how soon will he need a place? If it is several months away, you will not want to keep your rental vacant for that long. Down time for a rental means no income. Sometimes if a tenant looks especially good, you can work out a deal. For example, a tenant wants the house, but your rental house is ready to rent in July and he doesn't need a place until August. You can have the tenant pay for a half-month's rent in July, with access to move stuff in early. This makes it worthwhile for you to hold it for him and allows him to lock up a good rental. He is paying a half month's rent extra, but you are losing a half-month's rent by holding it for him. It's a fair agreement, and might be worth your loss to get an exceptional tenant.

During this initial phone call try to give the tenant information about size, costs, what utilities are paid, and when the rental is available. You can give them the address so they can drive by to see the location and exterior of the rental. If your vacating tenant is still in residence, make sure to tell the looker not to disturb the tenant.

Then give the prospective tenant a date and time when the rental will be shown. Hand out rental applications at this showing instead of having to mail them out. Ask the tenant to mail the completed application to your address, which you can have printed on top of your application. This keeps tenants from showing up on your doorstep, which can make be uncomfortable if you are alone. Make it clear to mail the completed application as opposed to leaving it at the door of the rental. You don't want to have to camp out at the rental, or keep checking for applications there. When the applications start coming in, compare your telephone notes with the applications. Does the information match up? Who looks like a good fit for this rental?

Showing the Rental

Now you are ready to meet face to face—to bring the blind date and the beautiful rental together for a once-over, which cuts both ways.

It usually works best to wait until the rental is vacant and you have cleaned and repainted to show it to prospective tenants. This way you are in charge of how it looks and can show it at its best. Occasionally when you currently have a good tenant who has made the rental look great you can ask if it is OK to show the rental prior to move out. A rental can look better with furniture and wall décor. If the tenant gives permission try to schedule a showing for a weekend hour and make sure to keep an eye on the possessions. When this works, it can get your rental filled more quickly with less of a vacancy factor.

This approach has been known to backfire. I once got permission to show a house that I thought was in good order. When I arrived at the open house, I found laundry piled high on the coffee table, dishes in the sink, packing boxes jamming the hallway, and the children's sandbox dumped just outside the patio door where all the looky-loos tracked sand across the nice hardwood floors. Oops.

I used to make individual appointments and then let the tenant in myself. But in today's climate, especially if you are a woman, it is no longer safe to show a rental alone. And it was often the case that after making an appointment to show a rental and driving over there, then the prospective tenant just failed to show up. This can be very frustrating as you are left pacing around an empty apartment looking at your watch. What works best is to set a specific time to show the rental. Say at 1:00 on Saturday. This way I can go over to the rental with my husband. A Saturday or a Sunday afternoon the weekend after your ad has come out works the best. You have had the week prior when your ad was running to take phone calls and set up this showing with your callers.

We live and learn. I used to set a time from say 1:00-3:00 with staggered times to spread out the lookers. This approach backfired as the people came either early, late, or simply were no-shows which left us standing in an empty house for several hours just in case anyone showed up.

With a set time for your open house you can see a lot of prospective people at one time. You can also hand out the **Rental Application*** form at this time, which saves time and postage. And you can look the tenants over and ask them a few questions. They can also ask you some questions and get good look at the rental.

This arrangement of a weekend showing works well around people's job schedules. It also gives you a chance to see how their children behave. Do the kids race around the house, put their hands on the walls, and eat their sunflower seeds from room to room? Do they climb the back fence, pull leaves off the tree and fiddle with the sprinkler heads? Or is this a calm, quiet child who stakes out the rear bedroom as "perfect for me."

Meeting each person face to face is a nice way to start getting a feel for what kind of tenant he might be. Did he come on time? Think in terms of on-time rent. What is he looking for? Does your house meet his needs? Does he need a yard? Think children or pets. Will he take care of the yard? Ask if he owns a lawnmower. Does he really, really like the house? Think long-term tenant. How soon will he need a place? Think about your vacancy factor.

It is a plus if he asks pertinent questions of you like: "What utilities do you pay? What is the security deposit? Does it have air-conditioning? What type of heating is in place? How is the neighborhood? How is the neighborhood school? Are you planning on selling the house anytime soon?"

This little dance is the first step in matching the right tenant with your rental.

Advertising/Showing the Rental Checklist

- ❑ Create your ad.
- ❑ Place your ad in one or two newspapers.
- ❑ Make time to be by the phone while your ad is running.
- ❑ Speak to the tenant on the phone.
- ❑ Take notes about tenant while on phone.
- ❑ Set a time to show the rental.
- ❑ Show the rental.

- ❏ Ask questions of applicants.
- ❏ Hand out **Rental Application*** forms.
- ❏ Ask tenant to mail completed form to you.

You are the landlord…care to dance?

*This form is found at the back of this book.

Chapter 3

Selecting the Tenant

Rental Application

The undersigned makes application to rent housing designated as Apt. No. _____
Located at _____ City_____.

Name_____
Address_____
Phone number_____
Social Security Number_____
Driver's License Number_____

Have you ever been evicted? Yes_____ No_____.
        If Yes, please explain on the back on this application.

Do you or any proposed tenant for this rental smoke? Yes_____ No_____

Any Pets? Yes_____ No_____ If so describe_____

How Many in Your Family? Adults_____ Children_____

Proposed Occupants	Relationship	Age	Occupation

Do you give the landlord permission to do a credit check?
Yes_____ No_____

The applicant certifies that all information given in this application is correct.

Signed _____ Date_____ *

*This is from the **Rental Application Form**

How to Find the Perfect Tenant

Finding the perfect tenant is like a little like dating. First you need to decide what you just **can't** live with, and then you look for someone with the qualities of Mr. or Mrs. Right. Knowing what you **don't** want will help you know what you **do** want in a tenant. For example, you don't want someone who will trash your rental. You do want someone who leads an organized life and has basic cleaning skills. In the rental dating game, the right fit for the right rental is important.

I hate to break it to you, but there is no perfect tenant. There are some good ones out there though and if you're lucky and observant you can be a successful matchmaker. You might even make a few friends. Tenants live out their lives in your rental. Eventually you will see the whole spectrum literally from birth to death—with marriage, divorce, sickness and occasional unemployment thrown into the mix. Tenants are real people, sometimes at their best and sometimes at their worst through the years. In this past year two of our tenants have had babies and we have watched another two face a life and death battle with cancer. Life is real. One of our tenants has rented from us for over 40 years. Many have been our tenants for over 10 years. So when you select a tenant be mindful that it can be a long-term relationship lasting longer than some marriages.

While no tenant is perfect, your task as the landlord is to find one who is the best fit for your rental: one who can actually afford the rent; one who has the right number of children for the number of bedrooms; one who comes with good references.

References

Most tenants will tell you they have excellent references. This means that they can get their mother to vouch for them. The rental application will give you only a sketchy view of who they really are and what kind of tenant they might be.

Checking out a prospective tenant is fraught with perils. References are just the tip of the iceberg. They give only a hint of what type of tenant may lurk below the surface. Hopefully, all of those relatives the tenant listed as references will have something nice to say, especially if they want him to move out of the guest bedroom.

But what about the last landlord? He is in a tricky position. If the tenant in question is one he can't wait to get rid of, would it pay to tell the truth? Telling you *"I'm evicting him for trashing the place, dealing drugs, and not paying any rent for the past three months"* is not likely to get the problem tenant out of his apartment. And he can actually be sued for defamation of character if he reveals too much. A lot will have to remain unsaid, or left to your interpretation. It may go something like this:

Landlord: "I've only asked him to leave as I need to get in and renovate the space so I can up the rent."
Translation: *After his disastrous tenancy I need to completely rebuild the apartment. This is the easiest way to get him out without showing cause.*
Landlord: "He is very social."
Translation: *His place is party central.*
Landlord: "He starts a lot of projects without finishing them."
Translation: *He is not as handy as he says. He tore up the flooring 6 months ago and has yet to lay the tile I bought for him to put down.*

While a landlord has to be careful about what he says about a bad tenant, the other side is that it saddens a landlord to lose a good tenant. Now he will have to start the rental dating game all over again. But hopefully, the last landlord of the near perfect tenant will be a good sport and give you a glowing report, as will you when it comes your turn to let go.

The rental application and checking the references will only tell you so much. Sometimes you just have to rely on prayer, intuition, and your sense of smell to truly size up a prospective tenant. Say for instance that you want a non-smoker.

You ask, *"Do you smoke?"*

"No" he says. But he reeks of smoke.

You pause and give him "the look" while pointing out the cigarette package bulge in his shirt pocket.

He responds a bit more honestly. *"Well, only at work. Never in the house. I'm trying to give it up."*

He may actually smoke outside—until the first cold snap. And until then he will leave a trail of butts in the garden and next to the front stoop. After the first rain, the cigarette burns will appear in countertops or in the rug. He will never give up smoking under your watch. If he's not afraid of emphysema or lung cancer, your little agreement means nothing. Most likely his teenage children smoke too. He may at times be unable to come up with the rent, but he is never out of cigarette money. You will never be able to get the smoke smell out of the carpet and the drapes, or the yellow stain off of the walls. So plan on renting to smokers from now on. And up your fire insurance. You may need it.

Take the time to try and find out about how things went at the tenant's last place. You will be dealing with a tenant for a long time so it is worth a few phone calls and a credit check to find out any bad news up front.

My father-in-law was in his 80's when he rented a house to a sweet young thing who flirted outrageously with him and completely hoodwinked him. Mrs. Flirty listed no references, but assured Pops that she could be trusted. He let her and her family in and the first month's rent was the last he ever saw. It took another six months to get her evicted. We checked with her past landlord just before the court appearance and learned that she had done the same thing to him— a serial flirt and shirk.

Attitude counts when sizing up a tenant. Is he pushy, aggressive, demanding? It will only get worse after he actually moves in. I've had applying tenants ask if I would remodel a room to suit their needs, add on a patio, change the exterior paint color, take out the carpeting, put in carpeting, forego the security deposit, or lower the rent, all before they were even approved as a renter. Some tenants mistake a landlord for a personal genie who can make all their wishes come true for free. They confuse a landlord with Santa.

Naughty or nice? A tenant with a bad attitude will usually give you one too. One tenant, Mr. Macho, moved into our rental after his new girlfriend (our original tenant) first got a restraining order and then a divorce from her husband. When we had him sign the rental agreement, he told us that he was really somebody special. *"They think I'm a god in Fresno."* Without a trace of humility, he then informed us that if his new girlfriend stepped out of line with him, *"She's out of here next!"* This tenant was not one I would have selected. He just sort of oozed in with our present tenant and her revolving boyfriends. It didn't take long for Mr. Macho to start throwing his weight around. He refused to let the pest control person into his apartment to spray our building for ants thus invalidating our three-year guarantee. In no time at all he had all the neighboring tenants mad at him. One evening the police called asking us to let them into Mr. Macho's apartment as they had received a 911 call and then a hang-up from his unit. When we arrived with the key, the apartment was bathed in the red glow of revolving police car lights. The police unlocked the door to find the girlfriend cowering, afraid to open the door to the police. It seems her small child had dialed 911 by mistake. Anyway that was her story. Our story is that we were mighty relieved when shortly thereafter Mr. Macho told us *"Your apartment is junk"* and gave us notice. He took his attitude with him.

The Real Test

Is there a foolproof way to select a good tenant? Well, almost…check out his car. Is it neat and clean or is there a lifetime supply of stale French-fries, food wrappers, dirty clothes and half empty soda cups strewn about the interior? This is the way he will maintain your apartment. If he eats in his car, he'll most likely eat in the apartment living room over the brand new carpet, in front of the TV. He's great at multi-tasking as long as it doesn't involve clean up. Is the windshield caked with dirt with a half circle cleared by the windshield wipers for viewing? He doesn't do windows or probably any dishes either. Is the body of the car shrouded in dust with "Wash Me" scribbled in the dirt? He doesn't own a mop or a vacuum cleaner. With him you will discover just how deep ground-in dirt can really go. Does he have a little statue of a naked hula girl bobbing in the back window? Expect plenty of overnight guests. A child's car seat in grandma's car? Expect live-in grandchildren. Is the car rolling on bald tires with primered dents and mismatched bumpers? He's not only a bad driver, but he might have trouble coming up with the rent. Car repairs will either bleed him dry or he won't be able to get to work. Is the headliner hanging down just above the driver's seat? Expect sheets for curtains. Does the car interior reek of cigarette smoke? Don't believe him when he says he only smokes outside.

If the car is clean and neat with a minimum of chaos inside, you may have a winner. Someone who will wash his car will probably clean the toilet.

The car check can be invaluable, but only if you go with your first instinct. This is something I failed to do when I once rented to two women. They charmed me with a sweet little note expressing their love for my cozy rental and informing me *"We are through with men."*

"We just want to live a quiet life in that cute little house." gushed the two ladies.

My first clue that this might be a pipe dream should have been the beat up condition and bashed in passenger door of their dingy compact car.

"Oh, my ex-boyfriend got mad and kicked it in," admitted Wanda Bet *"but he's history."* Within six months Wanda was in jail, her fellow tenant had vanished, and Mr. History was living in our cute little house with a new girlfriend. All this happened without our knowledge or the benefit of a rental agreement with our two new tenants. We didn't even know their names. Nor did they pay any rent during their abbreviated tenancy. The car is your first CLUE especially if the ex-boyfriend did it in the side door with his foot. I should have gone with my first instincts.

Look Before You Leap

If you don't get a chance to check out his car, an even better bet is to check out the prospective tenant's current home. Gaining his current address from the rental application, you can easily drive by for a look if the property is in town. Is the lawn mowed? Is the front yard a wrecking yard for torn apart cars. If a prospective tenant looks promising, you can ask for permission to see inside their present home. How neat is the house? Are the dishes done? Have the toilets been scrubbed lately? Any pets? Does the house smell like smoke? How many beds are actually in the house?

I once drove by to check out the yard of a tenant who said that she loved gardening and would take excellent care of our rental landscaping. Her current front yard was a barren field of stubby grass that looked as if it hadn't been watered in this century. The bare dirt was littered with broken bikes and toys. Old toilet paper streamers hung from a forlorn tree that had a few limbs ripped off. But the piece de resistance was the huge 8-foot by 24-foot cargo container that she had parked crookedly in the driveway. When I asked her about it, Mrs. Brown Thumb told me with pride that she took the cargo container everywhere with her as she needed it for her many possessions. I was glad it wouldn't be parked in our rental driveway anytime soon.

I've learned that as a landlord, you should go with your first instincts, a look at his car and present home and your prospective tenant's track record. This means carefully checking his references and his credit report. A leopard doesn't change his or her spots. He just polishes his claws on your doorposts.

Getting it Right

Know what you Want

The first rule of tenant dating/selection is to know what you want. The tenant usually knows what he is looking for, but you also need to decide what you are looking for. Know ahead of time what you want and don't want for your rental. How many people would suit your unit? Will you allow pets? What about smoking?

Legally you cannot discriminate against tenants because they are not married, have children, are a single mom, or have ten people in their family. You can however screen for what is appropriate and safe for your rental. An upstairs apartment may be unsafe for small children. A one bedroom is not large enough to hold a family with five children. Houses sharing a septic tank may need to be limited to perhaps three people per unit.

If you do not want pets, be firm and say NO in spite of the begging.

(See Chapter 7) There is no point in a tenant with pets even filling out an application for a no-pets unit.

Determine if you will allow smoking or not. This is very important because once a unit has been smoked in it is very difficult and expensive to restore it to a condition that a non-smoker would want. White refrigerators can turn yellow. Walls will need to be washed with a detergent solution and then painted with a stain killer and sealer before they can be painted or else the tobacco stains will bleed through. Carpets and drapes need to be cleaned thoroughly to get the smell out. Even then the smell of smoke can remain. Just think of the last smoking (as opposed to non-smoking) motel room you tired to sleep in.

Smoking also poses a very real fire hazard. The constant presence of burning cigarettes and smoldering butts always has the potential for fire. Many fire deaths are caused by a person falling asleep in bed or on the couch with a burning cigarette. This is a danger not only for the smoking tenant, but also for other tenants in your house or apartment building. No landlord wants to endanger tenants or lose a building to fire. There is also the concern that landlords have some obligation to eliminate the risk of harm to tenants from secondhand smoke. The tenant smoking under another tenant's window or by their doorway, for instance, exposes a non-smoking tenant to toxic smoke. For these reasons, smoke free buildings are becoming more popular. Law does not prohibit a smoke free policy.

Checking the References

It pays to take the time to check out the references your prospective tenant gives on the application.

Call the previous landlord first. This is the person who really knows if the applicant is a Dr. Jekyl or a Mr. Hyde. Ask the following questions about the tenant: Why is he moving? How long was he there? Did he pay the rent on time? How much rent did he pay? Did he have any pets? Did he smoke? How did he keep up the yard? Did he get along with the neighbors? How did he leave the place? Any problems with this tenant? Is this an eviction? If so, why? One of the best questions to ask the past landlord is: Would you rent to this person again?

Keep in mind that the previous landlord has mixed feelings in talking to you. If this tenant is really great, he will not want to be losing him. The landlord might secretly hope that the tenant will not move after all. If the tenant is a creep, the landlord is only too eager to see him find another place to live. How can he answer your questions honestly and still get rid of the baggage?

So you have to read between the lines. I once had a landlord tell me only, *"He paid the rent on time…that's all I'll say."* I took this to mean, *"I'm afraid of being sued if I say anything bad about this tenant from hell."*

A really good tenant may elicit glowing reviews from a generous landlord. *"He left the place better than he found it,"* is about as good as it gets. Other words you'd like to hear are: *"He always paid early. He really fixed up the yard. His kids are jewels. I really hate losing him as a tenant."*

The mixed reviews sound something like this. *"He starts a lot of projects, but doesn't really finish them. He has a lot of parties. He usually pays on time. We've only had a few problems. He only rented from me for a few months. We've had a few tangles. He's unhappy with the neighborhood. He wants a place where he can have pets."*

If the tenant lists no past landlord to check with, you are at a disadvantage. He may be moving away from home for the first time. He might be going through a divorce. He might be lying and doesn't want you to talk to his landlord because he's left there on bad terms or is being evicted. People usually don't go from owning a house to a rental unless something major has happened to change their lives.

Another reference it pays to check is the place of employment. Does the person really work there? How long has he been there? Is this a full-time position? Is he making a salary sufficient to pay the rent? Some questions may not be answered due to privacy issues, but it doesn't hurt to ask.

Personal references are only valuable if you know the person listed as a reference. This can happen in a small town. Then you know if the person giving the recommendation is someone whose opinion you respect. Unknown friends of the prospective tenant will usually say something nice, but they haven't rented to your guy, and might be hoping for a cool place to party.

You don't need to check the references for every application you receive. Some applicants may be simply rejected by you as an inappropriate tenant. This can be for a variety of reasons ranging from their perceived inability to pay the rent to the number of occupants being too many for the size of your unit. You only need to take the time to check references on those tenants you are seriously considering.

A **warning** is however needed here. In our litigious society, it is best to never state a reason for rejecting a tenant. By not stating a reason for rejecting a tenant you prevent both hurt feelings and a potential lawsuit. Angry applicants can threaten to take you to court if they feel they have been discriminated against for any reason—be it race, number of children, marital status, or even age. It is your rental and you have a right to decide who will live there. You will have valid reasons for not wanting to rent to certain people. However when rejecting an applicant, it pays to be a little vague and just say that you are still taking applications. After you have signed with a tenant you can then state that the unit has been rented. End of Story.

Doing the Credit Check

While it is a bit of a hassle, always do a credit check for a tenant who looks promising. The best way to get an unbiased view of your prospective tenant's financial outlook is to pay for a credit check. This way you will know if he reasonably has enough finances to pay the rent, if he has ever been evicted and has a judgment against him, and if he has filed for bankruptcy. You will need to have the person's permission to do a credit check. For this reason, a space asking for the tenant's permission and his agreement to pay for the credit check is included on the **Rental Application.*** I let the tenant know that I will only do a credit check on someone I am serious about renting to. An earnest tenant with nothing to hide usually won't mind paying for it.

The three main agencies for credit checks are: **Equifax** (at Equifax.com), **TransUnion** (www.transunion.com) and **Experian** (experian.com) You can order reports on line or use their 800 phone lines.

The easiest way is to have a rental company who does credit checks run it for you. You can have it faxed back to you in less than an hour. It usually costs from $10 to $25 to get a credit report run by a rental agency. You will need the tenant's social security number for this, as well as their signature OKing the credit check. These items are included in the **Rental Application*** form. You will also need some proof of ownership of the property like a utility bill. Or you can call a credit check agency to do the work for you.

Sometimes the most glib and confident applicant can be a scam artist. OK, so I'm skeptical, but the occasional con man gives you a phony application and nightmares thereafter.

We had one tenant with difficult to check references who looked great up front. He owned his own business, supposedly had family in town…so we let him in without a credit check. After the fact—in the middle of the eviction for non-payment of rent—we found that there was no guy with his name and social security number. He had no credit history. He had given us a false identity. He skipped out owing us and everybody else in town. It's too late to unlatch the barn door and shoo out the jackass once he has possession. Do you homework now or regret it later.

What to Look For

Some things I look for in a tenant are stability, a good fit to the rental, and the tenant's ability to easily pay the rent.

Tenant Stability

I want a long-term tenant, so I am looking for one whose situation is relatively stable. A married couple is usually more stable than a single person. The single person might move in boyfriend or girlfriend, get married, move out with a boyfriend or girlfriend or have a lot of parties. Or he might be a very quiet tenant who is easy on the rental. A person going through a divorce is in a very unsettled condition. He or she might reconcile, move back in together, or decide to move out of town. He can be in your rental one day and out the next. A new boyfriend or girlfriend might be part of the picture. Kids might come to visit or to stay.

Probably the least stable situation is the young person who has a first job and is moving out of home for the first time. He will most likely want a roommate to help pay the rent. Said roommate may or may not work out and may or may not move in a boyfriend or girlfriend who is of course "just a guest." (See Chapter 4.) Novice renters often have only a dim idea of the necessity for cleaning the toilet, doing laundry, watering the lawn, keeping harmonious relationships with neighboring tenants, and month-to-month financial planning.

When a tenant's life changes, your life changes. A rolling stone may gather no moss, but you want a rock-solid boulder for a tenant who will stay put and pay the rent.

A tenant is more likely to be long term if the rental fits his family and his needs. A family with four kids will be best in a home with at least three bedrooms. A guy who likes to work on cars will do best with a garage. The gourmet cook will want a good-sized kitchen. You don't want a tenant who can *make do* with your rental for a short time. You want one who says, *"This is perfect!"*

Suitable Job, Travel Time to Work, and Good Fit to Area

Travel time to work is also a consideration. If the tenant works at a firm a two-hour drive away, does he really know what he's getting into? What seems like a scenic drive now, may become a reason to move in a few months. Beware of the tenant who has yet to find a job but knows it will be easy to get. Get the job first, apply later. Also think twice about the tenant who is new to the area. Your town may not be what he thinks it will be, and greener pastures might call. A good prospect for a happy camper is the person who says, *"I just had to move back to My Town. I love it here!"*

Able to Afford the Rent

Next, I try to determine if the tenant will be able to afford the rent. This seems rudimentary, but if a tenant gets in over his head, you'll become the life preserver. You need to look at monthly income, the stability of the job(s), the ages and number of kids, the age of the car, and calculate if the total picture looks good. The tenant who is over-reaching financially can quickly start in with the late rent and the excuses. A car repair or a holiday can mean you don't see the rent. Sympathy is nice, but in reality you need to find the tenant who can actually afford to live in your rental. Otherwise it gets messy real fast.

Trust Your Intuition

Never disregard you own intuition. Sometime you just get a bad feeling about a person. Once I just didn't feel right about a certain tenant. My husband thought that the proposed tenant measured up great on paper, so we went ahead and rented to him. It was a big mistake. The tenant had lied to us in some crucial areas and things went downhill fast. The situation involved paranoia, a terminal illness, death, a meth lab, smoking in a smoke-free apartment, apartment damage, and moving in unauthorized guests. It ended badly with an ugly eviction. I should have listened to the little voice that said *No Way* early on.

On the other hand, sometimes your intuition says that this tenant would be perfect for your rental, even though they're had some problems in the past. We've taken a chance on a person based on this intuition and created a win/win situation.

Take Your Time

Lastly, take your time. It is better to lose a month's rent than to be saddled with a bad tenant. Often a tenant will say during the open house, *"We'll take it!"* and offer money on the spot. Resist the temptation to make any decision until you have checked references and credit. If you don't find a tenant who looks right to you—keep on looking. Run the ad for another week or another month. Show the rental a second time. Don't let a pushy tenant pressure you into a bad decision. When it comes to choosing a tenant, haste makes not only waste but also usually a date with an eviction attorney.

When you have found the tenant you want, the one closest to perfect, it is time to have him sign the rental agreement (See Chapter 4.) **Don't take any money until you have made a firm decision and signed the tenant.** Some tenants will beg you to take some up front money even before they have looked at the place. Taking money is in itself a binding legal agreement, so do so only after the rental agreement is signed and you are actually ready to enter into a legal contract with this person.

Selecting the Tenant Checklist:

- ☐ Check the tenant's references, especially his last landlord and employer.
- ☐ Do a formal credit check.
- ☐ Check out the tenant's car.
- ☐ Check out the tenant's present home.
- ☐ Is the tenant stable?
- ☐ Is the tenant a good fit to the rental?

- ❑ Can the tenant afford the rent?
- ❑ Pay attention to your intuition.
- ❑ Don't make a rush decision.

You are the landlord…never date someone you wouldn't consider marrying.

*This form is found at the back of this book.

Chapter 4

The Rental Agreement

Rental Agreement
Month-to-Month

This agreement has been entered into on the _____ day of _____ 20_____. It is by and between _____ Owner (Landlord) and _____ Tenant (Resident)

In consideration of their mutual promises, the parties agree as follows:

The Owner rents to the Tenant and the Tenant rents from the Owner for residential use only the premises known as:
_____, _____ _____.

| Street Address | State | Zip Code |

This agreement may be terminated by either party after service upon the other of a written 30-day notice of termination of tenancy. Any holding over thereafter will result in the tenant being liable to the owner for **rental damages** at the fair rental value of $_____ per day.

The premises shall be occupied only by the following named person(s):
(Include birth date if under 18.)

| Name | Birth date | Name | Birth date |

| Name | Birth date | Name | Birth date |

Guests.

Anyone not listed above who spends considerable time at this rental or who spends the night there is considered a guest. The maximum stay for any guest is to be three days per year. Anyone staying longer than this may do so only with the express permission of the Owner. This permission should be asked for well in advance of the visit and should be limited to rare occasions.

If the Tenant wishes to have another person not listed in his rental agreement live at any time in this rental property, the Owner must first approve it and the new Tenant must sign a lease agreement. Moving any person not listed in this rental agreement into the rental without approval will be considered a serious breach of this agreement.

No Subletting

No portion of said premises shall be sublet nor this agreement assigned. This means that the Tenant may not rent out any room or portion of this rental at any time, nor can the Tenant turn his lease over to any other party. Any attempted subletting or assignment by the Tenant shall, at the election of the Owner, be an irremediable breach of this agreement.

Trash

Trashcans are provided for the use of the Tenant. Your trash day is_____.

The Tenant should take his trash cans out to the curb each week prior to trash pickup time and move them promptly back behind the gate or wherever appropriately stored as soon as possible after the trash had been picked up. The tenant is not to leave the trashcans out at the curb.

The Tenant is not to let any trash build up in the house or on this property. If the tenant needs additional help in disposing of trash, please let the Owner know.

Apartment Landings

The upper landing of each apartment needs to be kept clear for easy Tenant access to the surrounding apartments and for fire safety. For this reason, no furniture, tables, chairs, potted plants, Bar-B-Ques, wind chimes, tools, brooms, flags, bikes, hanging decorations or other objects can be allowed on the landings, or hanging from the roof beams. Small doormats on the floor are OK.

Laundry Room

The laundry room is for Tenant use only. Visitors may __not__ use the laundry facilities at any time. Please follow the laundry room rules to keep the machines in good working order. Remove clothes promptly from the washer or dryer when done and wipe out the machines and clean the lint filter after each load. If the Tenant want to reserve a specific laundry time and day, he may do so on the sign up sheet posted in the laundry room.*

These sections are from the **Rental Agreement and the **Addendum to the Rental Agreement***

Spell It Out Now or Regret It Later

It is easy for things to get out of control in your rental. You had pictured life with Ozzie and Harriet. Instead, you seem to have gotten Ozzie Osborne. The lawn is unmowed. Broken toys and unread newspapers litter the driveway. Trash, broken furniture and malfunctioning appliances overflow the carport. The stairs and landings are crowded with dying potted plants and dangling wind chimes, making access nearly impossible. Music blares into the night. Cats and dog have turned your nice yard into foul furrows. The one bedroom house you rented to a single now has five cars regularly parked in the driveway and who knows how many people parked inside. What happened?

Chances are, you, as the landlord, assumed too much and didn't spell out enough in your rental agreement. These real life scenarios give you a glimpse of why no detail is too small to include in your agreement. Everyone has differing standards. Unless you spell out your expectations now, your tenant might have some expectations of his own which run contrary to law, common sense, or the landlord or neighbor's sensibilities.

The portions of the rental agreement included at the beginning of this chapter are some areas which are not covered in other chapters, but which I have found useful to spell out. The full **Rental Agreement*** is included at the end of the book for your use.

Guests

Take guests for example. Your tenants will. They will take them in for a few days…a few months…or even let them take over the entire rental when the original tenant moves on. This can leave you, the landlord, wondering, *"And just who are you?"* This is not a question you want to be asking, because anyone in possession of your rental has certain rights whether they are signed onto your agreement or not.

We decided to address the issue of "guests" in our rental agreement after Wanda moved in her boyfriend. I tried to be compassionate to her plight, as Wanda's husband had died just six months before. I wanted to give her a chance to get on her feet financially and emotionally. I began to lose sympathy, however, after the third hot rent check. I came to realize that she was not in heavy mourning, but seemed to be hot and heavy with the new man in her life. If I am going to support someone, I prefer to know his name.

We informed Wanda that her guest of four months had worn out his welcome with us and had to go. She herself was on shaky ground as she was three month's behind in her rent. She didn't budge and neither did her guest. Wanda informed us with a tone of righteous indignation, *"He's just a guest and I'm entitled to have a guest in my own home."* At this point her "guest" had been living rent-free in our apartment for four months. His personal checks (which bounced just as high as hers) were printed out listing our apartment as his address. I had to evict both tenants to get rid of Wanda and her "guest" and to get back in control of our apartment.

Mr. Suave, a single dad, rented a three-bedroom house from us where he wanted to raise his two children. Our first sign that all was not well was the appearance of a full sized mattress on the floor of the living room. Why would he need a mattress in the living room when he had bunk beds in one room for his sons and two additional bedrooms as well? Mr. Suave seemed to take our questioning as an over-reaction on our part. *"It's just for a friend who'll be staying for a few days. He's just a guest,"* he said coolly. Pretty soon the mystery guest was answering the phone and the door and we saw a small terrier running around in our "no pets" house. We never did find out the full story. But by the end of the eviction, our non-smoking house was trashed with cigarette butts in the fireplace and outside as well. The vertical blinds were scattered around the back yard and one closet door had gone missing. The "guest" was in possession of the house longer than our tenant. When the mystery guest finally left, black trash bags of garbage were left oozing on the front walk. These situations can cause a few emotions to ooze from the landlord as well.

The first time renter, especially a young unattached person, is the most likely to move extra people in to help pay the rent. When the realities of rent, utility payments and the cost of groceries fully hits, this tenant will often open his door to others who are willing to buy the pizza and are looking for a place to hang out. We once rented to Bud and Guy who wanted to room together while they worked part time and finished school. Their apartment quickly became a flophouse for all kinds of young men who slept on the sofas and drank beer on the stoop. Weekends, the place became party central as young women joined in the festivities. In spite of the non-stop houseguests and partygoers, Bud and Guy fell onto hard times financially and we were actually thrilled when they gave us notice. Too many guys drinking Buds for us to handle.

Getting It Right

The Rental Agreement

The rental agreement is your most important document in renting out a house or apartment. It spells out your responsibilities as the landlord as well as the tenant's responsibilities. This tells your tenant up front exactly what you expect him to do and **not** do if he rents from you. This doesn't mean that a tenant will always abide by the terms of the agreement, but it is the legal basis for your business relationship as landlord and tenant. This is a legal document which gives you grounds for eviction, should that become necessary, as well as a basis to get a judgment for back rent as well a court fees.

It is important to spell out the exact terms of the tenancy in your agreement. You want to cover everything from the amount of rent and when it is due to the breaches of the rental agreement that will be considered as ground for eviction.

The Addendum to the Rental Agreement

An **Addendum to the Rental Agreement*** is another way to spell out certain areas of the agreement in greater detail. An addendum "adds" to the more simple wording of the **Rental Agreement***, and expands on your expectations for the tenant. What do you mean by a guest? How late is late for the rent? What do you want done for yard upkeep? What vehicles will be allowed? What pet maintenance is the tenant expected to do? What business uses are <u>not</u> allowed?

Don't assume that the tenant necessarily knows what terms like *residential use only* means. To try to clarify each of these items in the rental agreement would make it overly cumbersome. I use an **Addendum to the Rental Agreement*** to spell out these issues. The tenant signs this **Addendum*** as well as the **Rental Agreement***. This avoids having the tenant come back and say, *"You never told me I couldn't raise goats in the backyard…do childcare out of the house…have my Cousin Elmer and his 6 kids spend a few years living with us."* Not only have you told him, you've told him in writing and had him acknowledge receiving this information with his signature.

Many of these issues are dealt with in subsequent chapters. This will be an overview and a look at some areas of the agreement areas not covered in the rest of this book.

Yearly or Month-to-Month Agreement

You need to decide if you will have the tenant sign a *month-to-month* rental agreement or a *yearly* lease. Each has advantages and disadvantages.

If your tenant signs a month-to-month rental agreement, you can evict him for any reason after the first month with a 30-day notice. If your plans for the rental change, or you realize he will not be a good tenant, you have no long-term obligation to your tenant. On the other hand, with a month-to-month tenancy, your tenant has no long-term obligation to you either. He can give you a thirty-day notice at any time and be on his way. After he has rented from you for more than a year, you are, however, required to give your tenant a 60-day instead of a 30-day notice if you want to evict him.

A yearly lease commits the tenant to stay in your rental for a least a year. It also commits you to allow him to rent from you at the current rent for that full year. Under a yearly lease you cannot increase the rent during that time. It is also harder to evict your tenant during that time, even for a breach in the rental agreement. A black and white eviction issue like non-payment of rent can be grounds for an eviction during the year's lease. However, a more side issue—like if he has a dog or not—will need to be proven to a judge in court. This can be pretty hard for you to substantiate as can proving if the tenant has extra people living there, if he is smoking in your rental, or if he is disturbing the neighbors.

A government-subsidized rental-housing contract like HUD also puts you into the year lease category. You are required to sign a year's lease in accepting a tenant on the program. The landlord is guaranteed a portion of the rent from HUD so that part it is more secure for you. However you still need to get the tenant's portion of the rent. A problem tenant is a lot harder to get rid of under the HUD program, except for non-payment of rent, once you have signed this lease. Except for non-payment of rent, or an extreme violation of the agreement, you are locked into the first year and need to give a 90-day notice for an eviction after the first year.

I would recommend going with the month to-month tenancy. This makes it a lot easier to evict a problem tenant and even to increase the rent. While a year's lease looks good for getting a long-term tenant, we have had even our best tenants break their lease without batting an eye. They decide to move out of town, buy a home, or experience a life change like a divorce. There is really nothing you can do if they decide to leave. Your year lease is pretty useless except to tie you to a legal yearlong obligation.

One tenant broke his lease with us and bought the house next door. He then dismantled our fence to make it easier to move his furniture from back door to back door, instead of going up and down neighboring driveways. I guess if you can break a lease, breaking down a fence is nothing.

Going Over the Rental Agreement & Addendum

Always take the time to go over the **Rental Agreement*** and **Addendum*** with the tenant prior to having them sign the agreement. Go over both agreements item by item to make sure that the tenant knows exactly what he is agreeing to. This eliminates any surprises on either side.

If the tenant was planning to run childcare out of your rental, for instance, or wants to have regular overnight visitors, these issues can be dealt with up front before the agreement has been signed. Emphasize that each point is important to you as the landlord and clarify items if the tenant has any questions. This way if there is an area that he is unable or unwilling to comply with, you can hopefully find out before the contract is signed. It is better to stop the deal now than to find out major differences in expectations later. It takes about 45 minutes to go over the **Rental Agreement*** and **Addendum*** with the tenant. I think it is worth every minute.

I always fill out two copies of the **Rental Agreement*** and the **Addendum***, one for me and one for the tenant. This way they walk away with a copy and I have the all-important copy for my file. If you have a copy machine, you could just make a copy for the tenant.

Giving Possession

When the agreement is signed you should receive some money to firm up the commitment. I usually take at least a $500 nonrefundable deposit. This proves the tenant is serious and you are not turning away other prospective tenants only to have the signed tenant back out. If you are signing the tenant just as he is scheduled to move in, you can collect the full first month's rent plus the security deposit and give him the key—which means you are giving him possession. Only give the key out if it is time for him to take possession and the total amount of up front money has been paid. Always have the tenant pay the first month's rent and the security deposit with a money order, cashier's check or with cash. You don't want to give someone possession of an expensive property only to find 10 days later that his check has bounced. If you let a tenant in without collecting all the money owed, especially the full security deposit amount, it will be much harder to collect it later when there is not as much of an incentive for your tenant to pay up.

Subletting

Do not let your tenant sublet your rental to anyone else. It is hard enough to stay in charge of your rental when you are calling the shots. Your tenant does not have the vested interest in protecting your property, your carpets, or your toilets that you do. When thinking of subletting, he only cares about the money part. He could actually start making money off of your rental if you let him start renting out rooms or the whole place while he travels to Europe, takes a vacation, or gets ahead financially. You are providing him with a residence, not a new career.

Make it extremely clear to your tenant exactly who you have allowed to live there. Any changes need to be approved by you and a rental contract with you must be signed by any new tenant(s) prior to their move in.

Once a tenant (approved or not) is living in your rental unit they have certain legal rights. It may not seem fair that you can end up supporting a stranger, but legally you cannot shut off water, power, or force him to leave your rental except through a legal eviction process. If you have no legal agreement with this person, he has agreed to nothing—especially not to paying the court costs of getting him out.

Only agree to additional tenants if you really see that as a good thing for your rental. People who are not related to your tenant have a way of coming and going like a bad rash. And you are left with the scratching.

Guests

To clarify the guest issue, I have limited the stay of any guest to three days per year. This way the tenant cannot argue that the person who has been there for a month is just a guest. I require that if a tenant wants to have someone stay there for longer than three days he must first get the landlord's written or verbal permission. This may sound a bit like elementary school, but believe me; you need to be firm on this issue. Otherwise you will quickly lose control of who is living in your property.

For instance, if a tenant wants to have his parents come for a three-week visit, it is usually OK with me. They probably won't be staying. But I don't allow boyfriends, girlfriends, adult children, or long-term guests to move in without my approval and without signing a rental agreement. This is for your legal protection. You want to stay in charge of exactly who is living in your rental. Remember that any person living in your rental has some legal rights to stay there.

One tenant, Ms. Hospitality, could not seem to come to grips with this portion of her rental agreement. In the course of her tenancy she moved in, at various times, her two sisters, their six children, various boyfriends and ex-husbands of said sisters, her brother and other relatives looking for work. The final straw came when she started renting out the back bedroom to a male friend who used the bedroom window to climb in and out of the apartment at all times of the day or night. Ms. Hospitality's door as well as her windows was always open for family or friends in need. We finally had to nail them shut with an eviction.

Keeping it Safe and Sanitary

Everyone has his own standards of cleanliness and safety, but even though you don't live there, your rental is your property and you are ultimately responsible for its condition. A laissez faire attitude with your tenants is likely to reap an *anything goes* result. And some tenants can go pretty far.

Trash can pile up at alarming rates. The garage can become home to splitting sacks of old clothing, broken toys, discarded TV sets and used refrigerators. None of these useless items is likely to go when the tenant goes. A stored refrigerator is a real liability for you as young children have died after they accidentally locked themselves inside a refrigerator and suffocated. If you do allow a stored refrigerator or store one of your own, make sure it is secured tightly shut with a locked chain.

The decks of your apartments can quickly sprout bar-b-ques, potted plants, hanging ornaments, chase lounges, chairs and cute little tables. When the tenant waters the potted plants they drip onto the heads of the tenants below and rot the boards on two levels. The carports accumulate used mattresses, discarded furniture, old tires and drained motor oil lurking precariously in an overfilled bucket.

To prevent things from getting out of hand, it pays to state some simple rules up front. Nail down what you expect for the apartment landings, the laundry room, the carport, and in handling the trash.

Trash

Always pay for the trash service at your rentals. Do not trust that the tenant will find this a necessity. While a tenant is unlikely to do without a telephone, he might decide to save money by just putting the trash outside the back door for the last few months of his tenancy. The only thing worse than this scenario of moldering old trash bags oozing who knows what out the broken seams is the unplugged refrigerator which has not been cleaned out either. A delight for at least three of the senses!

Discuss where the trash cans should be kept during the week, and the tenant's responsibility to take the trash out prior to pick up. Have him bring the trash cans back in from the curb promptly. Go over any recycling program you have in your area.

Let the tenant know that you do not want a lot of trash or junk to accumulate on the property. Tell him you will help him to get rid of used appliances or extra trash. Check periodically and don't let these items accumulate on your property. A nice rental property and a junkyard are just a few auto bodies and broken appliances apart. Talk turkey with your tenant if his standard of upkeep is not the same as yours.

Decks and Landings

Most tenants have an abundance of stuff. You need to have some say in where the stuff can be kept, especially if it affects neighboring tenants. That is why I have developed strict rules about what can and cannot be kept in such areas as carports, and the landings of our apartments.

One woman, Miss Ivy, decided to make her portion of the upstairs landing into a little haven. Her deck space was about 3'x2' if you didn't count the part needed as a walkway for the tenants down the hall. She crowded her space with over 50 potted plants, some of which hung from the rafters and bonked the other tenants on the head as they tried to pass to the stairs. She added a little table with two chairs. She added a few statues and a wind chime and a little glass angel. Her broom and mop also competed for space, as did a patriotic flag. The final touch was a wooden lounge chair, which caught the shins of unsuspecting passer's by. They tried to pass by. Their front doors were located past the masses of leaves and statuary. It was like a jungle up there with tempers growing upstairs and humidity increasing downstairs. Water dripped from her plants through the boards of the landing to form a mossy puddle at the doorstep of Apartment A below. My other tenants were about to bring out the machetes when I laid down the law. It all had to go. Miss Ivy was not happy. But her fellow tenants were. Since then I don't leave the outside decorating to chance or to the sensibilities of the Miss Ivy's of the world.

I now allow only a doormat on floor of the landing and nothing to be hung on its beams. No plants, barbeques, wind chimes, mops or furniture allowed. Not only does this provide harmony among the tenants, it allows a safe access for everyone. A bonus it that it makes our apartments look a lot neater and gives easier access for painting or repairs.

The Laundry Room

The laundry room is another hot spot of steamy intrigue. Tenants forget their clothes in the washer for days. They leave bleach crystals clinging to the tub, which attack the formerly black, best slacks of another tenant. They have only a vague idea of the need to clean the lint filter.

One tenant, Ms. Clean, monitored the laundering habits of my many apartment tenants. She knew just who neglected to clean the lint filter after a load of fluffy towels, and who had jammed too many blue jeans into a wash cycle. Mostly she knew who left the laundry room in a mess, and whose sheets had hung on the line for three days, thus causing Mr. Nice to accidentally back into the trash can due to his impaired field of vision. Ms. Clean knew who had put a load of sweaters in on Apt C' s day and whose loose change was likely caught in the agitator. I developed some laundry room rules and a new respect for Ms. Clean who struggled to make the laundry room safe for humanity.

Carports

Carports are another area where lines can be drawn in the grease if some firm boundaries are not set up. You'd be amazed at how much junk can be crammed in around a car. Discarded mattresses, used motor oil, furniture, old tires, boxes and bags, bikes and barbells can be stacked in precarious piles spilling out into the neighboring spaces. This accumulation of stuff is also an attraction for rats and stray cats. Most of this stuff is just stored and not used by the tenant.

To combat this problem we had lockable storage boxes build at the head of every carport. The tenant can supply a lock if desired. Tenants are only allowed to keep in their carport space one car, whatever will fit into these storage cabinets, and a bicycle(s). Nothing else can at any time be stored on top of the cabinets or in the carport space. I allow a bicycle or two, as those are hard to store in an apartment.

Again, this may sound stringent, but it has worked like a charm. The carports stay neat and clean and the tenants find that they don't need to save everything. If they have a lot of stuff they need to store they can rent storage space somewhere else. You have to stay on top of this by checking from time to time and asking tenant to remove anything that oozes in. In the long run all the tenants benefit. They can all have space to get into and out of their cars and don't have to endure the smell of rats or dusty junk.

In case you are feeling softhearted, remember—most of this accumulated stuff is basically useless junk, which will be left behind by the vacating tenant for you to dispose of. Better to get the tenant to get rid of it as he goes along than to have to haul and pay to dispose of his used tires later.

I wish I could work this same magic with the garages of tenants who rent houses, but that might be going too far. Since a garage is not a shared space, at least the mess is their own to deal with.

The Rental Agreement as a Legal Document

The **Rental Agreement*** is a document which is key to establishing the ground rules of your rental relationship with your tenant. It is the only legal document you have which sets forth the obligations and limits of this relationship. Do not lose this document. Make sure it is signed and dated. Keep it in a safe place.

From time to time you may need to refresh you own or your tenant's memory about a certain area of the agreement. If I have to write a letter to a tenant trying to get them to comply with a stipulation of their agreement, I refer to it by number and section. This way the tenant is reminded that he has signed a legal agreement saying he would or would not do a certain action while in residence in the rental. This has a stronger feel than just saying you would like him to do thus and so.

You can say something like the following: *"According to your rental agreement, which is a legally binding document that you signed on date_____, you have agreed to do thus and so (have no pets, not smoke in this rental, have no long-term guests, etc.) according to Section ___ which says_____. You are currently in violation of this portion of the rental agreement. Continued violation of this agreement is a breech of this rental contract, which is grounds for eviction."*

Having the full spectrum of terms spelled out legally also becomes a necessity if it comes down to an eviction proceeding. The first thing the eviction attorney wants to see is a copy of your rental agreement. Remember that this is a business and no matter how friendly and cordial your relationship with your tenant is, it is defined in the eyes of the law first and foremost by your **Rental Agreement***.

Rental Agreement Checklist

❑ Decide if you want a month-to-month or a yearly rental agreement.

❑ Use a good **Rental Agreement*** like the one at the back of this book that spells out all areas of the agreement.

❑ Use an **Addendum*** to clarify your expectations.

❑ Go over the **Rental Agreement*** and the **Addendum*** point-by-point with the tenant prior to signing these agreements.

❑ Only give possession of the rental over to the tenant after the **Rental Agreement*** is signed and dated and the full first month's rent and security deposit has been paid.

❑ Do not allow a tenant to sublet.

❑ Have firm guidelines about guests, sanitation, and trash.

❑ Have rules for the use of carports, decks and landings, and the laundry room

You are the Landlord...get it in writing. Written boundaries beat wild speculation any day of the week.

*This document is found at the back of this book.

Chapter 5

Rent

Rent

Rent is due in advance on the 1st day of each and every month at $_____per month, beginning on the _____day of _____ 20_____.

Late Fee

Rent is due on the first of each month. It is important that the Owner receive the rent on time each month in order to pay the bills on the rental. A five-day grace period on paying the rent is extended to the Tenant. Any rent not received by the 5th of each month will be considered late and will be subject to an automatic 5 percent late fee. This fee would be due and payable with the late rent. For example, the late fee on a $1000 rent would be $50 for a total late rent due of $1050. The purpose of this late fee is to encourage the Tenant to pay rent on time. Continued late payment of the rent will be grounds for eviction.*

This is an excerpt from the **Addendum to the Rental Agreement. This form is found at the back of this book.*

Those Darn Excuses

I used to believe what tenants told me when the rent didn't come in on time. I wanted to believe them. I felt their pain. After all, these poor people were very sick, or out of work, or ill-treated by an ex-spouse who withheld the child support payment, or out of town on a life or death matter. How could I expect them to worry about something as mundane as paying the rent? But pretty soon their pain became my pain. Their many excuses did not excuse me from being the responsible party. I was the one paying the price…and their water bill, and their mortgage, and their insurance. I noticed that these cash-poor tenants found the money to buy new cars and take expensive vacations. What was going on here? What was going on was the very human proclivity for a person to get away with what he can.

Your good tenants will never give you a moment's worry when it comes to the rent. They will get that check in the mail in a timely fashion. Their rent check will always be made out in the full amount of rent due and will never come up "insufficient funds" at the bank. If a true emergency keeps this from happening, they will hand deliver the rent within the 5-day grace period along with an apology.

But a few of your tenants think that the rules don't apply to them. Sure, they agreed to pay the rent on time, but the first of every month just kind of sneaks up on them. They don't really care that their mortgage, insurance, property tax, repairs, and water and trash bills have to be paid out of the rent they are supposed to be paying, or that you as the landlord will be assessed a penalty on any late payments. The tenant still expects fresh water to come out of the tap even when no money has come out of his pocket to pay for it.

When the rent doesn't come in on time, you make a phone call asking why you have not received the rent. This is when you hear the first of those darn excuses.

The number one excuse, of course, is *"The check's in the mail."* Yeah, right! In my experience, the Postal Service only loses rent checks that were never mailed. I know this because these checks never arrive. If all the promised rent checks actually did arrive in my mailbox one day, I really would be rich. I have spent days in good faith checking my mailbox, only to have the tenant admit later that he lied about having mailed the check in the first place.

Other excuses follow. *The car broke down. I've started a new job. My boss didn't pay on time. My child support payment is late. I was working late and couldn't get to the bank. There was a holiday. I was away on vacation. I got married. I got divorced. I didn't know it was the first. I've been sick. My child is sick. My dog has been sick…*by now you are starting to feel sick.

You will hear most of these excuses only after you have called and left numerous messages. The rest of the excuses come later, after the check bounces.

I tracked down one non-paying tenant just as she was leaving on a vacation to Hawaii. She claimed that she had given her half of the rent money to her roommate who had spent it on drugs. That, of course, absolved her from any responsibility for the unpaid rent. Too bad, so sorry. Aloha.

Another tenant bought a brand new car. The dealer wanted to receive payments on the first of the month. Since this would have put Mrs. Minivan in a financial crunch, she resolved this problem by shifting her rent payments to the 15th of each month. It worked for her.

Teddy called us over to his apartment to check a leaky faucet. Since his rent was already late, I enquired about it. *"Oh, darn,"* said Teddy, *"I can't pay you right now as I left my checkbook at the office"* I just happened to know that Teddy's office was right down the street.

"Why don't we just walk on over and get it?" I suggested. He then admitted that he had no funds to pay the rent. After some discussion, Teddy agreed to be out by the end of the week.

A single tenant had always paid the rent on time. One month his rent just didn't come in. He didn't return my calls. The house was dark. He seemed to have dropped off the face of the earth. He finally resurfaced at the end of the month from a honeymoon in Jamaica. *"I'm a little short on money,"* Mr. Newlywed said. *"I'll pay double rent next month."*

Coming Up Short

One stalling tactic used by tenants in financial trouble is to pay only part of the rent. Rufus began to have trouble paying his rent. He would drop by with $100 toward his $1000 a month rent. Later another $250.50 would roll in. Rufus always promised that payment in full was just a few days away. I had to start a separate ledger to keep track of his erratic payments. I made sure to fill out a receipt for each payment with the amount still due. (See the portion on record keeping at the end of this chapter.) This ploy of course confounded any way of charging a late fee and kept things constantly on edge. I spent time typing up letters detailing what was paid when, and how much still owed. I mailed them to Rufus hoping to elicit a payoff. When the case finally ended up in court at the end of an eviction, Rufus had the nerve to accuse me before a judge of shoddy record keeping. *"It just got so confusing,"* he said. *"I lost track of what I owed."*

Lucy made an innocent or maybe a not-so-innocent mistake. She transposed the numbers of the amount of rent owed and paid not $954, but $945. I informed her of her error and asked for the missing $9. I never got it. After several months of stewing over the $9 she had shorted me, I decided that sleeping at night was worth a lot more than the money Lucy owed. I forgave the debt in my mind, if not on paper.

The most pathetic excuses are the ones you hear after the check bounces. *The *&###@** bank made a big mistake. I swear the money is there. I'll get them to apologize to you. Do you need a note? I'm changing banks…they have messed up for the last time.*

I hate to get a check back marked "Insufficient Funds." Not only does this mean that my bank account is short that amount, but this usually signals the beginning of the end for a happy relationship with your tenant. Mistakes can happen, but a tenant who will write you a hot check is a real hot potato. You are the one likely to get burned.

After several bounced checks from the same tenant, I hand-walked Mrs. Short's latest check to her bank to see if it could be cashed. The teller checked and said there was not enough money in the account to cover the check. As I did other errands around town, I came across Mrs. Short in the park. I mentioned to her that her check was refused for "Insufficient Funds" and reminded her that it was a crime to pass bad checks, even to a landlord. She became indignant and insisted that her check was covered.

"I was just at your bank five minutes ago." I said. *"They wouldn't give me a penny."*

Mrs. Short insisted, *"They've made a mistake. I swear the money is there!!"* When the check comes up short, the bank is always the villain. Those bankers just don't know how to add. I was very tempted to suggest we walk together back to Mrs. Short's bank, where they were sure to believe her.

Getting it Right

Setting the Rent

The first, thing to decide is how much rent you will charge for each rental unit, whether it be an apartment or a house. Rents should be based on what units are going for in your area as well as the investment you have in your rental property.

A rule of thumb you often see used is that you want to get 1% of the market value of your rental each month. This gives you a 10% profit on your gross income per year. The one percent for ten months gives you the ten percent, and the remaining two months of the year go for things like insurance, and taxes. In other words, if you have spent $200,000 for a rental house, you should expect to charge 1% or $2000 per month.

The Going Rate

You may have a lot invested in your rental, but the reality factor is that you can't expect to get more than the going rate. Houses especially are not likely to bring in the rent they need to give you a 10% profit. You might be lucky to get $1000 a month depending on the local market. Apartments are more likely to give you that 10% return. You can check the classified ads for rental houses or apartments in your area to get an idea of what similar units in your area are going for. You might also want to actually look at some of these comparable units to see how the area and condition stack up against your rental.

In some cases your rental might actually be an alligator as far as income goes, taking you into the swampy hole of a negative cash flow each month. If this is the case, you have to decide if the appreciation factor is worth it.

The Appreciation Factor

In a good economy property values will go up, or appreciate, every year. Your investment in property is then growing in value as well as providing a monthly income. Of course the only way to partake of the increased value, besides raising the rent, is to eventually sell the property. This is why it is called "investing" in real estate. You are invested financially and for a space of time.

Amenities and Location

Other considerations that affect setting the rent are how large the rental unit is and what amenities it has. A one-bedroom one-bath rental is, of course, worth less to a tenant than a 3-bedroom, 2-bath unit. Does your rental have a fireplace, a fenced yard, landscaping, a garage, a den, a swimming pool, a view? Do you pay for any utilities, provide a gardener? All of these items add to your rental value. The part of town and the city where the rental is located all affect the rental market prices.

Rental Subsidies

If you rent your unit to someone who has a low-income subsidy like the Area Housing Authority, this agency will determine the total rent amount allowed for your unit. This is based on fair market value, and the number of bedrooms and baths in your rental as well as what the family is eligible for. A small family might not be eligible for a three bedroom and so you would only get a two-bedroom rate if you choose to rent a three bedroom to them. The agency pays most of the rent and the tenant pays a portion of the rent depending on their income. This arrangement guarantees you receiving the governmental portion of the rent on time, but not the tenant's portion. This tenant may or may not be a responsible person. You also are required to sign a full year's lease with the tenant under this program. You will have to undergo yearly inspections of the rental property and make any requested repairs or upgrades.

The Vacancy Factor

Before counting on a set income from your rental, you also need to consider the vacancy factor. You will not have your rental rented at all times. Expect at least a month of down time between tenants. During this time you will not only be without rent, you will have the expenses of cleaning and repair. It is common for a rental to have a yearly 10% vacancy factor. Since we keep most of our tenants for longer than average, our vacancy factor has been much lower, around 3%.

Renting Under the Market

Another thing to think about before setting the rent is that sometimes by charging a rent that is a little bit under the market, you can keep a tenant on a long-term basis. The grass doesn't look greener elsewhere when you have the most reasonable land and lawn in the area. We have had some tenants stay with us for 20-30 years in the same unit. However charging too low of a rent can have the opposite effect. Low rents can sometimes attract the tenant with the most financial and other problems. Tenants used to a very reasonable rent often don't appreciate the good deal they have been getting and may resent any rent increases.

When is the Rent Due?

Next you need to decide on when the rent is due. Since payment on most of your rental related bills will be due by the 10th of each month, I suggest sticking with a rent due date of the 1st of each month. It can quickly become confusing if you have more than one tenant and they all pay on a different schedule. Don't try to be too accommodating. The tenant can usually find some way to pay on the first. It is more appropriate for the tenant to juggle his finances than to ask you to do so. After all, you have the mortgage, insurance payments, taxes, repairs, and some of the utility bills to pay on each rental. You need to have the rent money in hand to cover these expenses.

Pro-rating the Rent

One problem in asking for rent on the 1st is that tenants may first move into your rental at odd times during the month. You would probably, if possible, like to rent your unit on the 20th of the month rather than wait until the 1st of the next month to let your tenant into that vacant house or apartment. It is 10 days more rent for you. But rather than start rent payments on the 20th and being stuck with that as the rent due date for the length of that tenancy, I suggest still collecting rent on the 1st. To deal with the odd number of days in their first month, you can pro-rate the first month's rent for the number of days the tenant will actually be in possession. Divide the monthly rent amount by the number of days in the month and multiply that amount by the number of days in the month the tenant will be in the rental. This is your pro-rated amount.

For example: A tenant comes in on the 15th of the month in a 30-day month at a rental rate of $1000 per month. Divide the $1000 monthly rate by 30 days for a daily rate of $33.33 per day. The tenant will be in the unit for 16 of the 30 days (the 15th through the 30th). Multiply these 16 days times the $33.33 per day for a total due of $533.28. This is the pro-rated amount owed for the partial month of tenancy.

The only problem with this is that you are in danger of letting the tenant in with a very small amount ($533.28) plus the security deposit. This is an expensive house or unit you are turning over for his use. You really want to know if your tenant can come up with the full amount he will need each month and the security deposit before you commit to the deal. The way I get around this is to ask for a full months' rent plus the security deposit up front. I credit this amount for the full second month of their tenancy and then the tenant only needs to pay the pro-rated amount (for the actual days he was in on that first month) on the second month. We have switched payments for those first two months. At the third month we are up and running at the regular amount from then on. Most tenants are fine with this arrangement. I write up these terms clearly on the rental agreement so there is no misunderstanding.

Can the Tenant Afford the Rent?

I always ask a prospective tenant, *"Can you afford the rent?"* I want the rental to be a good match to his needs and his ability to pay. Even when he says yes, I don't take his word for it. I check his application for income and any outstanding financial obligations to see if I think he can afford the rent.

Sometime a first time renter is overly optimistic. He may not realize how many expenses there are to day to day living. He may soon decide he needs a roommate or a less expensive place to live. If a tenant cuts it too close financially, the first bout of car trouble or unexpected doctor bill puts him and you into financial trouble. It always pays to check with the tenant's last landlord to see if he paid the rent on time. A credit check is your ultimate tool to see if he is a good prospect. (See Chapter 3 for more information on how to do a credit check.)

Collecting the Rent

Always be sure to get that very first payment of rent and the security deposit in cash, a money order, or in a cashier's check. A personal check is only as good as your new tenant's unknown bank balance. If this initial check bounces after the tenant has taken possession, you are in big trouble. Even an unpaid tenant in your rental has legal rights. So play it safe. I never give out the key until this full first month and security amount is paid and I am satisfied that the money is secure. (See Chapter 14 for information on the Security Deposit.)

Let the tenant know how and where you would like to receive the rent each month. Tell the tenant that he is responsible to get the rent to you on time. For me a check sent in the mail to my home is fine as long as it arrives within the five-day grace period. Rent is due on the 1st but I allow the tenant has a grace period up to the 5th of each month for the rent to be received before it is considered late. Most tenants mail a rent check. Tenants can also hand deliver their check personally to my house or they can pay in cash if they call ahead to be sure I will be home to write out a receipt or receive the check. Some tenants don't have a checking account. When they pay in cash, I use a receipt book that has numbered receipts and gives me a duplicate for my records. I do check any $100 bills with a forgery pen just in case, as the last one with a counterfeit bill loses.

I find it best **not** to try and collect the rent in person. It is a risky and time-consuming business to go door to door asking for the rent. Why should you try to catch the tenant at home in possession of his checkbook and a good mood? It is a setup for confrontation. You could also be a target if others suspect you are carrying lots of cash.

Bounced Checks

What happens when a rent check bounces? You deposited the check and then found out 10 days later in your statement that the check had bounced. When this happens, I call the tenant and ask him to bring the rent over in cash with the bank fee for the bounced check. If this happens once, I consider it a freebee. I don't assess a late fee. Anyone can make a mistake with the checkbook balance.

But if it continues to happen, then we have a problem. If I suspect that the next check might bounce as well, I take it to the tenant's bank in person. This saves 9 days of suspense by finding out right away if the check is good or not. If this check turns up insufficient funds, I have a talk with the tenant. It is illegal and fraudulent to knowingly write a hot check. If the tenant wants to avoid an eviction, he must pay up right away in cash. If this happens and the tenant stays on, I tell him that all rent payments from now on need to be in the form of cash or cashier check and must be on time.

The Late Fee

You like to believe your tenant can and will pay the rent on time, but then one month the first and then the fifth of the month comes and goes and no rent has arrived. What now?

This brings us to the **late fee**. Once you have set the rent, and moved your tenant in, what do you do when he doesn't pay the rent on time? This is one of the major frustrations in your life as a landlord. You are expecting the rent. You are counting on it to meet your rental bills. When it doesn't arrive on schedule, it upsets your financial and emotional world. One thing you can count on as a landlord is not to count on responsible payment of rent.

While you want to have compassion toward the harsh realities in your tenant's life, you don't want to be played for a sucker. Paying the rent should be a priority. The bank doesn't care about your tenant's hard luck when it comes to receiving the mortgage payment in full. But some tenants just can't seem to pay their rent on time.

So what can you do about it? Behavior modification is best left to the experts, but you can make use of the well-known idea of the carrot and the stick. Some Landlords with many units have encouraged on time payment of rent through a tenant lottery. Once every six months the names of those tenants who have had on time rent payments are put into a hat and one is drawn out to win a trip or some other great prize. If you can't afford to offer a sizable carrot as a reward, there is always the stick.

This is where the late fee comes in. If there are no consequences for paying the rent late, some people will always pay late. A tenant will make his car payment on time as he don't want his new SUV to be repossessed, but if he can put off paying the rent, it is worth getting a phone call from you. A late fee makes it a bit more painful for the tenant to pay late. Paying the rent late now costs him money, instead of just causing you, as the landlord, frustration. The late fee cannot be considered as rent owed in an actual eviction proceeding, but it is a good way to encourage on-time payment of the rent.

Assessing a late fee usually works toward getting the tenant to pay on time. But not always. Sometimes a tenant will just refuse to pay a late fee. Don't tell your tenant, but short of an eviction there is not much you can actually do to enforce this part of his rental agreement.

For some, the late fee is seen not as an incentive to pay on time, but as interest worth paying for extending their rent payment timeline.

One tenant began to pay the rent late including the late fee on a regular basis. Sally had it all figured out. The first month she included a note, "*My paycheck was held up because of the three-day weekend, so I paid late, but it's OK because I included the late fee.*"

The next month Sally wrote: *I had a few problems and with that and the holidays, money is tight, so I included the late fee. Don't cash my check until the 15th.*

I had to inform Sally that rent was still due on the first and the late fee was meant as a disincentive—not a license—for late payment.

Chronic Late Payment of Rent

Consider evicting a tenant who is chronically late in paying the rent. The situation is unlikely to get any better and will be a monthly source of frustration for you. At best the late paying tenant is a thorn in your pocketbook and a trial to your patience. You find yourself making idle threats and pleading phone calls. At worst, the late paying tenant starts getting free rent from you. He slides into making the rent payment on the 15th of the month, thereby getting a half-month of rent-free. Then he slides a whole month behind. Now he has achieved a full month of free rent. He may never catch up.

Even worse, once a tenant starts having trouble paying the rent, you're probably on the road to a forced eviction for non-payment of rent. Time is money. The sooner you get rid of a bad tenant the better. Non-payment of the rent is the single most common cause for an eviction. If the tenant can't pay the rent, he probably can't pay the electric bill, the gas bill, or a lot of other things needed to keep your rental in good condition.

Lottie had her electricity turned off for non-payment. Her worried neighbor called and asked me if I knew that she was burning candles in her apartment at night for light. I hate to think what she was doing for heat.

Business or Charity?

This brings us to the question of how long do you put up with late rent or no rent? Some tenants really are down on their luck. You need to decide if you can afford to support them. I believe that you get to choose the charities you support. When a tenant loses a job, or has a serious illness he is in big trouble. You feel sorry for him. But his trouble is not your responsibility. You have a business arrangement with him. He is not a family member who you will see through thick and thin. You are not his workman's compensation, social security, or health care provider. You do not receive government funds earmarked to help the unfortunate. Your tenant has not made insurance payments to your account.

As much compassion as you may have for his troubles, the bottom line is: did you agree to support him—to pay his housing, water, and trash? Did you agree to chip in for medical expenses? I don't mean to sound hard, but what a non-paying tenant is really asking you for is an unsecured, un-negotiated loan at no interest that will probably never be paid back. He is asking for a cash gift. You are not the bank. You are a landlord. You have bills to pay also and you need the rent check to pay them. An unemployed tenant can soon make you unemployed as a landlord if you don't take action.

I have to admit that this is the hardest part of being a landlord. You feel like a real schmuck when you say no. Case in point. A tenant called. Wendy was a single mom who worked hard to take care of herself and her handicapped teenage son. We had just agreed to let her move an older son into her apartment so he could help her with the rent. This son injured himself shortly after move-in and couldn't work, so now she had two sons to support. Wendy was calling because she had just been diagnosed with cancer. She needed surgery. Would I forego half of the rent for the next two months? Bam! Talk about putting you on the spot. I was just trying to absorb Wendy's terrible news. Then in the next breath she was asking me for a cash gift at my most acute moment of sympathy. Darn. I hate it when this happens!

I felt sorry for her—I really did. The compassionate part of me wanted to say, *"Oh sure…what are landlords for?"* But the realistic and experienced part of me silently noted that this might only be the beginning. Wendy was asking for a gift of a considerable amount of money upfront and if I gave her this money now in the form of forgiven rent, it would only delay the rest of the story. If I cut her rent in half now, then what about the next month's and the next? I swallowed hard and referred her to the local agency that was set up to cover this type of emergency. The agency helped her with the rent and saw her through the crisis.

It is always a judgment call. When a tenant can't pay the rent, you can give him a little time if you can afford it and believe he is acting in good faith. You can suggest he ask a relative for help. You can refer him to an agency. But there comes a point when you have to decide if you can afford to risk the continued nonpayment of rent. Eventually saying, *"If you can't pay the rent you will have to move out"* doesn't make you into a bad guy. It only feels that way.

Record Keeping

This brings us to the importance of Record Keeping. Having rental property is a business and needs to be run like a business. While you may be on friendly terms with your tenants, they are not your friends. Whenever money is involved, get it in writing and keep good records. Get a good filing cabinet and keep a good filing system. Your record keeping begins with the rental application and ends with the disposition of the security deposit. In between you need to keep records of:

- The Rental Agreement
- The Security Deposit
- The Social Security Number of your tenant
- Current telephone number of the tenant
- Information and rental agreement for any additional tenants who move in with the original tenant.
- Walk-Through Inspection Forms
- Painting and Maintenance
- Business License
- Business Tax Certificate
- Appliance purchases
- Yard Maintenance/bills
- Repair bills for your income tax
- Property Tax
- Utility Payments
- Insurance
- Rent payments
- Any eviction proceedings
- Forwarding address

These records are vital for your income tax records as well as any legal proceedings that may arise. If you are not organized, the lack of record keeping can raise up to haunt you. A tenant claims to have paid the rent. What proof do you have that he didn't give you cash? The window in the kitchen is broken. The tenant says it was like that when he moved in. Is he right? The stove moves out with the tenant. *"It was mine,"* he claims. Can you prove that the stove was your property? Your income tax accountant needs to know what you spent on utilities and repairs for each rental. Do you have the breakdown?

Raising the Rent

If you have had a tenant for over a year, you may want to raise the rent to keep up with rising expenses, inflation or the rates in your area. If the rent increase is less than 10% you need to give the tenant a 30-day notice plus 5 days for mailing. If the rent increase is over 10% you will need to give a 60-day notice plus 5 days for mailing. A rent increase must always begin on the day rent is due, not in the middle of the month. The **Notice of Rent Increase** form is found at the back of this book.

Some things to consider before raising the rent. If you raise the rent, you may lose a tenant who finds a better deal or uses the increase as a reason to step into buying the house he's been saving for. On the other hand, if you let your rents get too far behind the going rate, you will find it harder to ever catch up. Obviously, your profit margin will be greater if your rents stay ahead of your expenses, which tend to rise each year. Most tenants can take a small increase each year much easier than a large one every 3-4 years. The best time to make a big rent jump is when you are changing tenants. This way the tenant comes in at the higher rent rather than feeling that he now pays more for the same space.

Raising the rent is an emotional event. I can remember back when I was a financially struggling single mom and tenant. I cried when I received a rent increase. So I am not without sympathy for the plight of the tenant. Now on the other side of the fence as a landlord, I try to balance the need to make a profit with the need for kindness.

But no matter how kind you think you are, where money is concerned, the fur and the excuses fly. Your tenant will come up with all sorts of reasons why **you** are unreasonable in raising his rent. He is on a fixed income. He has been a good tenant. He has made improvements. Your tenant naturally sees things from his perspective. He really has no idea of how much you have invested in your rental. He doesn't have the foggiest notion of what you pay for taxes, for the plumber, or for insurance. The tenant only knows that a rent increase will tend to crimp his upcoming budget.

Usually these arguments against a rent increase take the form of a letter written soon after the tenant receives the rent increase notice. I have received letters four pages in length citing the poor economy, the tenant's financial poverty, and my implied greed as reasons to forgo increasing the rent. I have recently taken to responding by sending a chart published the newspaper, which listed the high, low and average rental fees in the county. The rent I'm asking is always far below the average and this is a high rent city. Sometimes this causes the tenant to be grateful for the break, but not always. Often it is the tenant for whom I have kept the rent the lowest who seems to appreciate it the least.

A tenant sees things from his point of view. He understandably wants to pay the lowest possible rent in order to use his money on other things. However, if your rentals are to be a business and not a charity, you have to make money in the deal. In an inflationary economy this means asking for a rent increase at regular intervals as your expenses increase.

We do sometimes keep the rent low for a given tenant as an act of charity. We have carried some tenants for years who pay less than half the going rate. We choose on occasion to do this to help others. However we cannot do this as a general rule and stay in business as a landlord. Raising the rent is painful for both sides, but in a growing economy it needs to be done.

One tenant for whom I had kept the rent the same over a 4-year period objected when I finally raised it by $100 a month. He was adamant that it would have been better to raise it slowly over the years. I had to agree with him, but I did the math and showed him that if I had done as he suggested he would have paid considerably more over that period than the increase was asking for. He had come out ahead on the deal by paying a lower rent for 4 years. He was not convinced.

Be aware that asking for a rent increase may bring other repercussions. It seems to open the door for your tenant to give you his *"Major Improvements I Want"* list. This often accompanies the letter protesting the increase. In the tenant's line of thinking, the extra money you will now be taking in should go toward improving his rental. He reasons that if he's paying more, he should get more. *I need a new stove. The paint is looking dingy in the bathroom. How old is this carpeting? I've been thinking how nice it would be to have a little patio cover....*

I often wonder if the tenant realizes that his "wish list" would often consume the total rent increase and then some for a period of several years. Add your growing taxes, utility bills and other expenses which were the reason behind the increase in the first place, and you could soon be going in the hole. Or you could increase the rent...which increases the wish list...which—well you get the picture. If you were planning on making some improvements to the rental, now is the ideal time to do so. But don't be bullied into expenditures you don't want or need at this time.

When you increase the rent, be prepared to see a few tears, and to get a letter protesting the change and requesting improvements. Your job is to be as kind as you can, to hold the line on spending, and if possible on your tongue.

Rent Check List

- ❑ Investigate what comparable rentals are going for in your area.
- ❑ Set the rent amount.
- ❑ Determine when the rent is due.
- ❑ Collect the first month's rent and security deposit.
- ❑ Pro-rate a partial month's rent.
- ❑ Explain how you want the rent paid.
- ❑ Decide if you will assess a late fee.
- ❑ Consider evicting a tenant who has trouble paying the rent before he gets too far behind.
- ❑ Keep good records of rents received and expenses paid.
- ❑ Raise the rent as needed to keep up with expenses.

You are the landlord...You're smarter than any banker. But remember, you are not the bank.

*This form is found a the back of this book

Chapter 6

Utilities

Utilities

The Tenant shall pay for all utilities, services and charges, if any, made payable by or predicated upon occupancy of the Tenant, except: _____ which will be paid by the Owner.*

This section is from the **Rental Agreement*

On Waste, Wattage and Water

It is usual for most landlords to pay for the trash and the water for their rental property. This works because you want the to keep trash from building up on the property and your want to encourage the tenant to water and maintain the yard. If times get tough for your tenant, these are areas he might choose to forego.

On the other hand, you probably don't want to pay for the utilities of electricity and gas as these bills can go sky high if the tenant doesn't have to pay for his own usage. Paying the piper, or in this case the electric company, at its escalating rate has a way of curbing irresponsible energy use. Nagging by you is not likely to produce the same effective result.

Sharing a Meter

We have two little rental houses on the same lot, which share an electric meter. This made for a lot of bickering between the two tenants when it came time to split the bill every month. Each claimed that the other was leaving lights on unnecessarily or running too many loads of wash. One tenant refused to pay his half. The other tenant balked at paying a larger part of the bill even if he had a larger family. To make the peace, I finally agreed to pay the electric bill for both houses and raised the rents slightly to pay for the increased expense which I estimated might be a high of about $45 per month per house. At first the bills came in at the expected rate. But when the colder days and nights of winter arrived, I got an Edison bill for over $200! This was $100 worth of electricity per house, and the heating was gas. The bill for my much large home for the same time period was $65. It seems that now that they didn't have to pay for the electricity my tenants began using electric heaters instead of the more reasonable gas wall heaters we supplied. They no longer needed to turn off lights or be careful in the use of appliances. Their total therm use tripled and moved into the high rate assessment. Thrift comes with paying your own bills.

Saving Water/Energy

The opposite problem happened when we had the tenant pay for the water at a nice rental house. Miss Thrift broke up with her live-in boyfriend and gave us a 30-day notice. I had no concerns about the yard as she and her boyfriend had always taken good care of the landscaping and had even put in some new trees and plants during their tenancy. It was a shock to take possession a month later and find that Miss Thrift had stopped watering the yard in the heat of August. She wanted to save some money. Never mind that we couldn't save the lawn, the flower or half of the hedge. Even a tree died of thirst.

Usually a tenant will keep the home lights burning and the heat on. He will pay the gas and the electric bill. If he doesn't choose to conserve, it's money out of his own pocket, not yours. However I once got a call from a concerned neighbor letting me know that a neighboring tenant had had her electricity and gas shut off for non-payment. *"She's burning candles for light at night!"* my informant said. *"I don't know what she's doing for heat."* In an apartment building, burning candles is a grave fire danger. Safety is an issue that must be addressed even when the tenant is paying or in this case not paying the bill.

Trash Collecting

Trash is another area of utility service where it is best to take responsibility. We even pay for hauling away excess trash and old appliances as they can quickly build up on a property. Letting trash accumulate at a rental is the first step to seeing it get trashed.

Mr. Fixit brought home all kinds of broken down appliances and used cars on their last tire rims. He had good intentions, but never actually fixed anything. He collected old soda cans by the back door and odd tires by the garage. When the TV went dim, it went into the garage along with old clothes, broken toys and decrepit sofas, listing on three legs. The only thing Mr. Fixit actually fixed was us when he moved and left us with enough junk to fill a huge dumpster and a small wrecking yard. All those free things he brought home didn't leave for free.

Other Utilities

Other utilities that you and your tenant must deal with are TV cable, and phone lines. Cable and phone companies will need your permission, as the landlord, to add extra lines. This is a good thing as a tenant in business for himself can quickly have lines curling like weedy vines out of the walls and across your floors. This jungle of phone and cable lines can leave you with unwanted holes in the walls and cables snaking across each room.

Getting It Right

Pay for Trash and Water

Decide which utilities you will pay for and which ones will be your tenant's responsibility. I recommend paying for trash and water. This will keep the grass green and the trash to a minimum. Let the tenant pay for gas, electric, phone, and cable TV. Be sure to make this clear in your rental agreement.

Keep Plumbing in Good Repair

The most important area of your utilities to keep in good repair are the plumbing items which includes sinks, toilets, tubs, showers, septic systems, and yard sprinkling systems. A leaking pipe or a running toilet can fill up your septic tank quickly. A dripping faucet will wear away the seat and necessitate replacement of the seat instead of just a washer. Also a drip can quickly become a steady stream. If the drip is from the hot water, the water heater will have to run all the time. This will create higher gas bills and cause the water heater to wear out faster.

A leaking pipe is another peril to ceilings and floors, not to mention the carpets. At one upstairs apartment we had a hard-to-find bathroom leak that was bubbling the ceiling of the bath in the apartment below. We broke into the upstairs wall and make some pipe repairs. We re-plastered the ceiling below. It bubbled again. A perceptive plumber finally determined that the caulking on the upstairs tub was not well sealed. A drip on the tub faucet above had run back to the wall and then into the ceiling of the apartment below. We paid dearly for one little drip.

Another time, a tenant in the downstairs apartment failed to let us know that the plumbing was backing up. Sandy never complained. She was not unduly alarmed when gray water began coming up in her downstairs bathtub whenever the upstairs tenant took a shower. It usually went back down, so she never called us. Never, that is until the night the tub filled and then overflowed all over the house. The water raced across the bathroom floor and flooded the living room hallways and bedrooms, totally ruining the carpets and buckling the hardwood floors underneath. It required a wet vacuum, total removal of the carpeting and padding, and three days of running fans to dry everything out. A few minutes with a plumber's snake could have averted this costly repair. I wish Sandy had complained sooner.

I have never had a rental, which needed a complete plumbing makeover. Usually it is just a matter of a clogged pipe or a leaking faucet. Ask tenants to report any leaks or stopped up lines to you right away.

When plumbing backs up, your tenant will want your backup ASAP. Learn the number of a good plumber. I have the tenant call me with a plumbing emergency to get an authorization from us to call the plumber of our choice. This way if the situation just needs a replacement washer, I can decide to have my husband handle it. Or I can OK the tenant to call and arrange for a time to let the plumber in. In a true emergency, if I cannot be reached each tenant has the number of the plumber to call.

To keep that hot water coming, you will need to replace the water heater when it gets old, preferably before it springs a leak and floods the garage, or worse yet the carpet in the house.

A water heater should last about 8 years. Buy a good quality of water heater. An apartment can use a 30-gallon water heater, but a house should have a 40 gallon one. The water heater will come with a pop off valve, which will release if the pressure builds up too high. You will need to add a downspout to take any water released down to the floor level. For a water heater located inside the house, you should have a drain to drain it to the outside in case of leaks. Each water heater should be strapped in so that it will not fall over in case of an earthquake.

If your rental is on a septic system you need to limit the number of people in your unit to what the system can handle. A septic tank should be pumped once every two years. This will keep it from becoming overfilled and clogging the leach lines. After pumping a septic tank, have your tenant flush the contents of 2-3 packets of dry yeast or another commercial product down a toilet to restart the bacterial action in the septic tank.

Water

Since you are paying for the water it is important to have some understanding with your tenant about water conservation. You want the yard watered, but not too much. You want the grass and trees to survive, but not to win the "most verdant yard on the street award." You don't want to be paying for your tenant's over watering or for water running down the street. Talk to your tenant about not forgetting and leaving the water on for too long, and ask him not to water overnight. In most areas water rates are on an increasing scale. If you use over a certain amount, the rates go up. Also a garden can be a real water sinkhole. You won't be getting any of the produce, just the higher water bills. You may choose not to allow a garden. (See Chapter 9 on Landscaping.)

Leaking faucets and running toilets are another major water waster. Be sure to instruct your tenant to let you know right away about any leaking water. Let him know that you are eager to fix the problem and prevent a high water bill.

Expect higher water bills in the summer months, but check out the situation if the bill seems too high. Look for leaks, running toilets, gardens, or overnight watering of the lawn.

Gas and Electric

When the tenant is paying for gas and electric, it is up to him to set up the account with the company. The gas company will turn off the gas between tenants, which necessitates re-lighting any pilot lights for wall heaters, the water heater and the stove when the gas is turned back on again. A Gas Company representative will usually handle this. Be careful that this relighting has occurred before your tenant moves in.

I sometimes have the electricity put into my name for a short period of time between tenants when I know that I will be needing to have work done on the rental that requires lights or electricity. Also, a house with no lights cannot be shown after dark. Just be sure that the new tenant puts the electricity into his name right away so you aren't getting the bills.

I Smell Gas…

Never put off checking out and fixing an electrical or gas problem in your rental. If a tenant smells gas or says there is a burning smell when he turns on a light, have it looked at right away. You need to be sure your rental is safe at all times.

As I was writing this chapter I got a call from a tenant saying that he had smelled gas in his unit and had called the Gas Company. The Gas Company serviceman had found a leak in the gas line and had shut off his gas at the meter. He recommended I call a plumber. So, sensing that fate was handing me another anecdote for this book, I paused in my writing and called our plumber. By noon all the gas lines to our six-unit apartment complex had been dug up and the plumber needed my permission call in a cement cutter to take out a portion of the sidewalk to gain full access to the lines. I drove over to access the damage. Dirt was piled high and the trench was rapidly filling with rainwater or was that sewer water? It smelled OK…. so I hoped he hadn't hit a sewer line. Even though only one gas line was leaking, all the lines were old and in need of replacement. The plumber chewed on a sandwich as we discussed options. I decided that while everything was dug up and the sidewalk segment coming out, now was a good time to replace all six of the gas lines. Gas lines are no place to scrimp. The plumber said he would try to have the job finished before dark. I was back in my car and halfway around the block before I remembered that all the pilot lights in each apartment would need to be relit after the gas was turned back on. I came back to the scene and asked the plumber if he could relight the stove, wall heater, and water heater pilots in each unit. He said he could, and I gave him directions as to where each appliance was located in each apartment. He was to call me if he couldn't get in to any apartment to relight the pilots.

The job actually didn't get finished until the next day. Only one tenant called to say she smelled gas in her unit. Her water heater and wall heater pilots had not been relit.

Bite the Bullet on Major Repairs

Major repairs of this type need to be made from time to time. You have to make some capital improvements like major plumbing repairs, replacing the roof, remodeling a kitchen or bath. It comes with the territory. Don't let these areas get too bad or dangerous before biting the bullet and making the repairs needed.

When it comes to rentals, you never know what a simple phone call will lead to, or how expensive it will be. Always keep an extra balance in your rental account. You don't know when an emergency plumbing or other repair might arise, and you'll need to be able to pay for it. Oh, I forgot, you are rich. Or maybe you thought you were until the last major plumbing repair.

Heating and Air Conditioning

A gas wall heater is a more efficient form of heat than an electric heater and is much safer than a portable electrical heater. Be sure that any gas heater has a good vent to the outside. If you provide central heating or air-conditioning this is all the more reason to have your tenant pay for gas and electric. An air conditioner left on all day can really make the electric meter run around.

Phone and Cable

In this wired generation, most tenants will want more than one phone line. But what if they want 20 lines? Who will be manning those lines? Is there a home business brewing? (See Chapter 11 on Rental Uses.) Stay in charge of the number and placement of phone and cable lines in your rental. Remember that when this tenant and his many TV's and computers moves on, you will be left with the holes in the wall and the damage to the roof from the satellite dish.

Record Keeping

Good record keeping will help you with the upkeep of appliances and utilities. Whenever you buy a new stove, water heater, wall furnace, air-conditioner, microwave, or even a sink or faucet, write it down with the date of purchase. This date is also needed for income tax purposes. I keep a card for each rental just for this information. List when major repairs or routine maintenance was done. This gives you a record of how old each item is and when it is likely to need replacing. Should you fix that faucet or replace it? How old is it anyway? Is the water heater on the way out, or might it just be a problem with the pilot? Is the air-conditioner two years old or twenty? When did you last pump the septic tank at your rental? A written record helps you make better decisions about replacement vs. repair and helps you ward off big problems by planning ahead for needed maintenance.

Final Notice

On occasion, especially after an eviction, a tenant will move out and the unpaid gas and electric bills will keep on coming to the rental mailbox. You are not legally responsible for these bills as they were incurred in the tenant's name. The tenant doesn't care if the electricity is turned off for non-payment, as he's long gone. But he may have trouble getting service at his new digs. Sometimes a disgruntled tenant will leave lights, air conditioning or water on after his move-out just to run up a bill he has no plans on paying. Check your vacant house as soon as possible after move-out, especially if you are putting the electricity in your name between tenants.

As a courtesy, to the utility company who, like me, has just been ripped off by my former tenant, I usually call the company and explain that the tenant no longer lives there. If I know a forwarding address I give it to the company and send the unopened bills to the tenant's new address, although it is unlikely he will pay them.

If you do not have a forwarding address for a tenant who has moved, you should return any of his mail unopened to the post office.

Utilities make your rental livable. Without water and heat and light it would be a cold world indeed. Your challenge is to make the costs of utilities livable for you. Limit which utilities you have to pay for and you limit your worries. While you are not responsible for paying for all the utilities, you are responsible to see that all systems are working and safe.

Utilities Check List

- ❑ Decide which utilities you will pay for. Trash and Water recommended.
- ❑ List the utilities you are paying for in your rental agreement.
- ❑ Keep good records of appliance, plumbing, heating purchases and maintenance.
- ❑ Talk to your tenant about water conservation and reporting any problems promptly.
- ❑ Keep plumbing, electrical and gas appliances in good working order.

You are the Landlord…you don't have to keep the light burning in your rental window, but you do need to keep the water on and the toilets working.

Chapter 7

Pets

Pets

*Only the pet(s) listed in your **Rental Agreement** may be kept at any time on this property. An outside pet is expected to remain outside of the house at all times with the exception of the garage area. The Tenant is expected to clean up any feces from this pet on a regular basis and not allow any odor to build up on the property. Any damage done to the carpeting, house, fencing, or property by this pet is the responsibility of the Tenant and repair expenses will be deducted from the security and/or pet deposit. Repairs exceeding these amounts will be charged to the Tenant.*

Any pet is to be kept reasonably quiet so as not to become a nuisance to the neighbors. Any pests such as fleas associated with the animal's presence on the property should be treated at the tenant's expense. Any additional pets may be kept on this property only with the express written permission of the Owner.

Pets agreed to at this date are:

_____

_____

_____

A pet deposit in the amount of $_____ was received on _____20_____.*

*This section is taken from the **Rental Agreement** and the **Addendum to the Rental Agreement**

Why Most Landlords Eventually Say "NO PETS!!!"

I consider myself an animal lover. But I've learned the hard way that new carpets and pets don't mix. Every prospective tenant describes his or her pet as quiet, sweet, and potty trained. His cat or dog is a trusted and indispensable member of the family. His pet is an exception to the rule and never barks, scratches, digs wets or chews. He has never seen a flea. He is willing to pay a pet deposit, but not one large enough to actually pay for new carpet.

What he forgets is that the landlord doesn't get to enjoy the finer points of his pet. We're left with the fleas. The part we usually see, or rather smell, is the pungent aroma of urine-soaked carpeting accompanied by a quick mental calculation of the cost for replacing the year-old carpet—again. Think I'm exaggerating? Here are a few true stories of property plundering pets.

Pet Stories

The Smiths, a young couple, begged me to allow their sweet little Siamese cat. We discussed litter boxes, frequent vacuuming, and flea treatments, and I gave in. After all how bad could one little cat be? A few months later, a plumbing emergency caused me to enter their apartment. The stench of cat urine and feces about knocked me off my feet. They had a litter box all right, but it was kept outside the back door. The cat was inside all day while they were at work and had used the carpet throughout the house for a toilet. In the end we had to tear up and replace all the pad and carpeting throughout the house and even replace the baseboards to get rid of the odor. The security deposit didn't come near to covering the cost of that one little not-so-sweet smelling cat.

One strange case involved the mystery of the wet floor. Mr. Wild rented a nice three-bedroom house from us. After five years of tenancy he called complaining that the floor in the middle of his carpeted office was soaking wet. The carpet was soaked in a five-foot area, and as it was summer, we couldn't blame El Nino. A series of plumbers looked for leaking pipes and even checking for pinhole leaks in the copper piping under the floor. There was no leak. In fact no pipes even came near that floor area and the wetness was not traveling from a bathroom or pipe connection. After three house calls from various plumbers with no answer, this was becoming an expensive proposition.

It was in a conversation with the latest plumber that I got my first clue. *"I think it might be coming from the watering bowl,"* he commented.

"What bowl?" I asked.

"That big watering dish for the dog. It was overflowing and had slopped water on the floor when I made that last house call." he said.

During my many visits the floor was devoid of any such doggie dish. Mr. Wild had an elderly yellow lab, which was supposed to be strictly an outside dog. When I questioned him, he admitted that he had been keeping the dog inside, as it was terminally ill with cancer. Why he chose to water it on a carpeted area as opposed to the kitchen vinyl flooring was another matter. Mr. Wild, however, was still adamant that this could not be the source of the problem. He said he was always very careful, and we were talking about a lot of water. Indeed we were. Mr. Wild had led us on one long wild goose chase. Later, when we pulled up the pad and carpeting, the hardwood flooring underneath was stained and warped from a long-time accumulation of wetness. By this time the poor dog had died, the water bowl was gone and the mysterious wet floor had dried right up. Of course so did our wallet, as we had to replace both hardwood flooring and carpet.

My mother probably has the ultimate pet/carpet story. One of her tenants simply fenced in a corner of the newly carpeted bedroom floor to create a cozy nursery for his dog to birth and raise her puppies on. The tenant didn't bother with niceties like newspaper or towels or cleanup. Now that's thoughtful!

Once, in a moment of temporary insanity, I actually allowed two outside dogs. Their owners, the Mutts seemed like nice folks when they rented the house with a lovely fenced back yard. It was a bit of a shock a year later when they divorced and vacated. Even more shocking was the state of the backyard. The lovely landscaping was now a moonscape of bare earth and furrowed holes. Worse yet, the bare dirt was littered with mounds of poop, probably the full year's worth, which took ten large trash bags and a breathing mask to collect. Thank you so very much.

Phantom Pets

Monty, a single tenant, had agreed to the "no pets" clause of his rental agreement. He was fussy about the appearance of his apartment but called me about an area of his light beige carpeting that was in need of cleaning after only two months of tenancy. Since the carpets had just been cleaned before he moved in, I wondered why they would need attention so soon. I went over to the apartment to check out the trouble. While Monty was bending over, pointing out the stained area on the living room carpet, a little white terrier trotted out from a bedroom, made for the carpet and took a dump directly on the soiled area. This was classic. I was supposed to pay to clean the carpeting due to an un-housebroken dog that wasn't even supposed to be there? I think not. With a little pressure, the non-existent dog and his owner left shortly thereafter.

Miss Moonbeam had an original way of thinking. Since she had agreed to "no pets" in her apartment, it was a shock to drive up one day and see a two by one foot pet-door cut and installed into the previously pristine hardwood front door. We reminded her of the "no pets" rule. She was totally unrepentant. *"I didn't think a cat was a pet,"* she said.

Phantom pets crop up in spite of the best lease agreement. Alex was a short-lived tenant of a small house. "No pets," he promised. When he moved out, a workman was called in to repair some broken windows. Immediately, fleas began to leap on him from the carpet and he had to flea bomb the entire house before he could continue working. Apparently Alex had kept a pit bull dog there. I guess bulldogs aren't pets either.

One tenant, in spite of agreeing to "no pets," got a puppy, which promptly chewed a hole in the middle of the hallway carpet. Another tenant adopted a stray kitten. This worked for him until he had to move elsewhere. Then he just left the cat, along with an ant-infested feeding dish and overflowing litter box, behind for us to deal with.

Miss Violet was reclusive. She disliked opening her door to us for even the most pressing of plumbing emergencies. Miss Violet would first spend time scurrying around the apartment shutting all the bedroom doors before we were admitted.

The "no pets" policy was in force, but I heard rumors that numerous cats were in residence. My need to let workmen in was rare, however, and I never saw a whisker. But when Miss Violet left, her four cats had left more than a calling card. The carpeting was hopeless. We pulled it out with gloves on and masks over our noses. The lovely old hardwood floor underneath was urine-stained in many areas to a dull black. Yes, pets are lovely! Just not the part I get to see.

Disturbing the Neighbors

Pets don't just raise your repair bills; they also raise the ire of the neighbors. We allowed one tenant to have a pit bull dog as the house had a large fenced yard. They cleaned up after Ying Ying and he didn't seem to do too much damage inside the house. I was doing some painting on the adjacent house one day, and noticed that a dog was barking and barking, howling and yowling, crying her little heart out. It seems that Ying Ying didn't like to be left alone. She was left alone a lot, the neighbors told us. She was not happy. They were not happy. An unhappy dog like Ying Ying can make maintenance difficult too. One day a fallen tree in the yard required us to come in and cut up and haul branches. Little Ying Ying wagged her tail and let us in at her owner's command. But every time I bent town to pick up a stick, she gave me a little nip on the rear.

Horses and Other Large Pets

Have rentals in the country? Bigger pets can bring even bigger problems. You could say they can really get your goat, sometimes literally. One property had a horse corral where we kept our little Arab mare. Our new tenant, Miss West, owned a horse and was paying big boarding fees elsewhere. For her the corral on the property was like a neighborhood gold mine. We were reluctant to move in a second horse until we figured out issues like liability, feeding, and cleanup. Not to be deterred however, one day Miss West just moved her horse in. Our Arab soon sported a bloody horseshoe-shaped wound on his rear. Miss West saved on boarding fees, but we had to consult a vet.

One rental house had an old barn, shed and corral. Given all that space, it seemed only natural to say "yes" to a horse, several goats and a few rabbits. Then came the questions. Who keeps the fence up, where do they put the manure, what about fly control? What about the rats that are being attracted to the grain and the wild cats living in the stored alfalfa? And why are the rabbits without water on this 105-degree day?

Large pets can create even larger problems.

Getting it Right

Pets or No Pets?

Now that you've heard a few pet horror stories, you need to decide if you really want to allow pets or not. Dogs and cats are your usual suspects. Usually a pet fish or a hamster is no problem. But when Okaying fish, do talk about aquarium size. A large aquarium may weigh more than your floors are prepared to bear. Also, a large bird like a parrot can create quite a mess and a lot of noise for the neighbors if kept outside or on a
porch. A tenant who keeps reptiles like a snake or a boa constrictor may have a chilling effect on the neighborhood.

Yes to Pets

The upside of allowing pets is that you will have a lot more applicants. Most tenants come equipped with a pet or two. They will be delighted to find a landlord who is a pet lover.

Be sure to spell out exactly what you expect your tenant to do in the way of maintenance. Much of this is written out in the excerpt from the rental agreement at the start of this chapter. No detail is too small to clarify. Inside or outside? How many cats? Does the tenant have a scratching post or will Blackie be using your curtains? Is your tenant planning to let the cat have a litter of kittens for the children's education? Is the dog neutered? How often will the tenant clean poop from the yard? What will he do to preserve the landscaping? If this is an apartment, where will the dog do his duty and who will clean it up? Will a cat box be used for little Fluffy, and how will the tenant dispose of the litter? How will he control fleas, barking, or keep a big dog from scaring the neighbors? Don't assume that your tenant has thought these matters out or that his standard for pet care matches your own.

Get a pet deposit up front in as large an amount as you think is reasonable or barring that, possible. Think in terms of how much it would cost for the following: replacing all the carpeting in the house: washing and repainting all the walls to remove the pet oil, staining and dirt: sanding the toenail marks from the hardwood floors and refinishing same; flea bombing the entire building; and replacing all the lawns and most of the landscaping. Worst-case scenario? Maybe, but it happens more often than you'd think and a $500 deposit doesn't go very far to cover those types of damage. The next tenant, even a pet lover, wants clean fresh smelling carpets, and a real yard.

If possible, go look at the place where your prospective pet-owning tenant lives now. How does his livestock interface with its present space. Any lawn left? Poop picked up lately? Complaints from the neighbors?

If you choose to allow pets, remember that for some animal lovers, the more pets the merrier. Spell out for the tenant the limits (i.e. only one cat) and the responsibilities (flea control, feces removal, carpet cleaning etc.) of bringing a pet or pets into your rental. Do periodic checks so there will be no harsh surprises upon move out like shredded vertical blinds or a years worth of accumulated droppings.

NO to Pets

Decided to say NO to pets? You'll save yourself a lot of grief, but be prepared to hear every sob story on the planet about why their pet is an exception. Your ad may say *no pets*, but that won't stop the begging. They will promise anything to move little Brutus in, but remember; when the last truckload moves out he may leave more than a few fleas behind.

Choosing to go *no pets* will cut back on the number of applicants you have to choose from, but it will also cut back on major cleanup and repairs.

Enforcing the "no pets" rule is no walk in the park either. While most tenants are great people, some will not bat an eyelash while lying to you about their pets or supposed lack thereof. For them, rules are made to be broken. They'll sign anything to move in and bring in the Bull Mastiff later on. Others want to change the rules a few months down the road. *"The children begged for a puppy…I'm just dog-sitting for a few days…My friend died and left me her long-haired cat…My parents are on vacation and I said I'd keep Bootsie and Puff Ball while they're in Europe for a few months…I didn't think an iguana was a pet…"* You'll hear it all.

The trickiest part of "no pets" enforcement is what you won't hear. The errant tenant is unlikely to pick up the phone to inform you that they've just adopted a pregnant cat from the shelter. It helps to have an undercover agent in the building or a helpful neighbor who will keep you updated on the goings on in your rental. This anonymous person is an invaluable aid to knowing what's up with your rental. Never, never expose the identity of your undercover agent to your tenant.

When renting to a new tenant, who promises "no pets," it's a good idea to do a periodic inspection, especially during the first year. Don't assume that all is well. Legally you are required to give a **24 hour Right of Entry Notice*** before entering your rental house or apartment. This requirement, of course, gives the devious tenant time to get little Fido out of the house prior to your inspection. You can however look for clues. Dog hair on the baseboards? Cat food in the cupboard? Chew toys under the couch or in the bushes? Cat litter in the dumpster? Pet carrying cage in the garage? Leash hung by the back door? They are bound to forget something.

In most cases, except for certain senior apartments, it is legal to refuse to allow pets in your rental property. If you refuse pets, your selection of tenants will be more limited, but so will your repair bills. You will be the bad guy…but get used to it. Be sure to let your tenant know up front that this is an important item for you and violation of this clause means eviction for them.

Pets Checklist

Pets Allowed

- ❑ Inspect the tenant's previous residence to see how pets and property are maintained.
- ❑ Collect money up front for a pet deposit.
- ❑ Specify number and kind of pets allowed.
- ❑ List pets allowed by name on the rental agreement.
- ❑ Specify if pets are to be inside or outside only.
- ❑ Discuss clean up and flea control.
- ❑ Discuss if dogs will be left alone outside and what they will do if the dog barks a lot.
- ❑ Inspect the property from time to time for cleanliness and upkeep.
- ❑ Check periodically on number of pets.

No Pets

- ❑ Go over the "no pets" clause of your rental agreement.
- ❑ Stress the importance of this issue.
- ❑ Inspect periodically for adherence to this clause.

You are the landlord…Pets are the stuff of your worst nightmares, and your tenant's pride and joy.

*This form is found at the back of this book.

Chapter 8

Vehicles

The Owner desires to keep this rental property free from any unused, abandoned, or superfluous vehicles. This includes cars, trucks, boats, trailers, motor homes, campers, motorcycles, busses, etc. To this end, the Owner asks the Tenant to keep only the following approved vehicles on this rental property or on the street in front of or adjacent to this property at any time. No one is to live at any time in a vehicle or trailer on this property. Any vehicle that drips oil or other fluids must be fixed or parked over a pan to prevent oil damage to the driveway or garage floor.

Vehicles approved at this time on the property are:
> *Make*   *Year*

_____

_____

_____

The following applies if the rental is an apartment with a carport instead of a garage:

The carport should be used to store one vehicle and anything that will fit into the storage cabinet. The Tenant may provide his own lock for the storage cabinet. Nothing else (with the exception of a bicycle) should be stored in the carport. The Owner wishes to keep the carport area neat and clean and to prevent attracting stray cats or rodents. To this end, at no time is the Tenant to store boxes, mattresses, tools, appliances, furniture or other items in the carport. Anything not fitting into the storage locker must be disposed of or stored elsewhere. This rule will be strictly enforced by the Owner.*

This section is from the **Addendum to the Rental Agreement*

The Garage vs. the Wrecking Yard

This section of the rental agreement may sound a bit overboard, but I've learned the hard way that unless strictly supervised, vehicles can overtake your property faster than crabgrass. Your yard can quickly become a wrecking yard littered with pulled engines oozing puddles of oil, old jalopies with flattened tires, and inoperable Junkers propped up on stacks of wobbly boards—their hoods open like gaping mouths.

Leonardo was an artist. What we didn't know was that one item he would use for a canvas was a large tour bus belonging to a rock band. He had a working commission to paint its 35-foot sides with artwork and the band's name all in psychedelic colors. Leonardo parked the hulking bus right next to our other tenant's houses and took his time with the airbrush. We got complaints. It seems that not only did the bus completely block out the daytime view, but Leonardo's artistic temperament functioned best at night. The roar of the air compressor, bright lights, hiss of the sprayer and smell of acrylic paint did little to lull his neighbors to sleep.

Trailers

Trailers are another eyesore. Somehow they arrive on your property but they never leave. Soon the tires are flat and the rusting hulk is used for junk storage. With a trailer there is always the danger that it will become housing for someone you don't know and don't want living on your property. Someone who will also be using the living room, kitchen, and the toilet and bath facilities in your rental house.

We once rented a small house to an elderly couple. A month after move in we noticed when doing a drive-by that there was a little trailer parked out back. It seems that the couple's son had moved in, along with his wife and three kids. Instead of two tenants, we now had seven. And did I mention the dog? It took an eviction to get rid of the whole kit, caboodle and poodle.

Cars Under Repair

Cars that are optimistically called "fixer-uppers" are another problem. They check in—are partially dismantled—and never check out. Various grime-laden parts are strewn about the yard and driveway. The gutted cars sit, like large dinosaur carcasses, dripping oil on the cement and adding to the overall beauty of your property.

Marty Mechanic liked to bring home old cars. His stable of vehicles included: a 1969 Pontiac missing a transmission, a 1974 Chevy pickup sans one door and most of the running parts, a 1982 Oldsmobile Cutlass without driver or passenger seats, and other assorted autos in various stages of disrepair. At one time we counted 8 vehicles in Mr. Mechanic's garage, driveway, and even parked across the street.

One tenant moved out but left a 100-pound front-end clip from a Camaro resting in the back yard. A non-functioning beat up six-cylinder 1976 Nova was abandoned in the driveway of another house. Used motor oil is another item that never moves out with the tenant. These are not easy items to dispose of for you either. Landlord/wrecking yard supervisor. Add it to your job title.

Unless you want your rental turning into a wrecking yard, try to keep control of the vehicles that wander onto your property. It is a lot easier to get the vehicles evicted while the tenant is still in residence and values his tenancy then to wait until they have vanished, leaving a few metal mementos of failed dreams behind.

Carports

Carports add to the opportunities to accumulate assorted car parts and clutter. Since carports are usually a shared space, each tenant's personal junk can quickly intrude into another tenant's space. And this is not to mention the negative visual impact of old mattresses, rusting bar-b-ques, broken toys, and sagging sofas that tend to accumulate there.

In our apartment carport, the mess became a health hazard. The unsightly accumulation of old mattresses and overstuffed chairs as well as boxes of clothes had become an attraction for neighborhood cats. They lounged and wet and pooped, as did a more secretive battalion of rats. Tenants complained that they couldn't get out of their cars because of the lineup of junk intruding into their space from the neighboring carport. At this point we declared war, and nixed the anything goes attitude in the carports. We first built large locking storage cabinets in the front of each carport. The cabinet doors, which could be secured with a padlock, prevented access by cats and rodents, and provided a secured and defined area for tenant storage. Then we laid down martial law. Nothing allowed in the carports except one car and whatever the tenant can stuff into the storage locker. We did make an exception for bikes, as they are hard to store elsewhere. Now not only are the carports neat and clean, but the tenants get along much better.

Getting it Right

Limit the Vehicles

Don't feel that you are being a Scrooge to limit the number and kinds of vehicles allowed on your rental property. Most tenants can get by nicely with one or two vehicles. They can also be remarkably creative at finding other places (besides your rental) to store that motor home or boat. Many neighborhoods have laws prohibiting the parking of large trailers or motor homes on the street in residential areas. Neighbors rightly object to hulking vehicles parked on the street that block vision and safe access to the street as well as their view. So unless the property has lots of off street parking, insist that your tenant find trailer storage elsewhere.

List the make and year of each vehicles allowed on the rental agreement. This gives you a record of the cars agreed to and allows you to ask for the removal of vehicles not approved by you on the property.

Car Repair/Oil Changes

Discuss car repairs and oil changes with the tenant. Make it clear that any car repairs done on the property are to be minor and not include lengthy and messy teardowns. Ask your tenant how they will handle oil changes. If they do it themselves, how do they plan to dispose of the old oil? Old motor oil needs to be disposed of legally through a recycling station like a Gas Station that does oil changes. You don't want oil being dumped down your toilets or in the street drains. Nor do you want old oil stored on your property. It is a fire hazard. Stored oil can also be spilled, ruining your garage floor or polluting your yard.

You may even want to stipulate that old tires are not to be stored on the property. These are usually left behind and you have to pay to dispose of them properly.

I also include a clause about dripping oil in my rental agreement. A car that is leaking oil can ruin a garage floor or a concrete driveway in short order. I ask that such a vehicle be repaired or a pan to catch the oil be kept under the parked car. This may sound petty, but a huge oil slick that has eaten away your asphalt devalues your property and makes it less attractive to the next tenant. There is no quick fix to repair an oil stain or damage. Putting down sand and scraping up old motor oil on my hands and knees in a rental garage is not my idea of a fun-filled afternoon.

Carport/Parking

If your rental involves a shared carport, consider building storage lockers and restricting what can be stored in the carport. You will need to check from time to time to enforce this rule, or things will creep into the carport space. I sometimes shift around the carport spaces among the various tenants. At times a large vehicle size or the need to access the passenger side is better served with a middle carport for example. For this reason I don't number the spaces to go with the apartments. This allows some flexibility. At one apartment building we don't have a carport space for every tenant. The tenants who forego a space pay a lesser rent.

If the tenant has more than one vehicle and your rental includes only one carport space per tenant, discuss where the additional vehicle can be legally parked. Most tenants don't mind their own vehicle parked in front of their front window, but tend to object to someone else's car parked in the same spot.

If a vehicle on your property appears to be non-running, ask about it. When a vehicle has been parked so long that the windows are dirt-covered and the tires are flat, it is unlikely to ever be repaired. This means that it will detract from your property and probably be left where it lies as a parting gift to you. Ask the tenant to remove it from the property while he is still in residence.

Vehicles Check List

- ❑ List approved vehicles in your **Addendum to the Rental Agreement***.
- ❑ Insist that trailers, boats and extra or non-running vehicles be stored elsewhere.
- ❑ Discuss car repairs.
- ❑ Discuss oil changes.
- ❑ Discuss tenant responsibility for oil dripping from cars.
- ❑ Discuss where the tenant can park.
- ❑ Discuss what can and cannot be stored in the carport.

You are the Landlord…Don't let any car-guy turn your rental into a wrecking yard.

This form is found at the back of this book.

Chapter 9

Landscaping

Yard Maintenance

Rental fees ☐ do ☐ do not include the services of a gardener. The Tenant is expected to assume responsibility for watering the lawn, trees, and plants and keeping them in good condition. The yard is to be kept reasonably weed free. If a gardener is provided he will mow the grass. If no gardening service is provided the Tenant is expected to mow the lawn every 1-2 weeks. No tree or plant is to be removed without the Owner's express written permission. Any plants put into the ground on this property become the property of the Owner and are not to be removed when the Tenant leaves. If the Tenant wishes to retain ownership of a tree or plant, it should be planted in a pot. No severe pruning of trees or bushes on the rental property is allowed without the express written permission of the Owner. The Tenant may maintain a small garden if space is available without removing any of the existing landscaping and with the permission of the Owner.

If the Owner is paying the water bill, it is expected that the Tenant will help by conserving water and not over-watering. If the Tenant's water bills become too high due to a garden, the situation would have to be reassessed to either discontinue the garden or to have the Tenant pay any portion of the water bill over a reasonable base amount to be determined by the Owner.*

This is a portion of the **Addendum to the Rental Agreement*

Landscape or Moonscape?

Maintaining the landscaping at your rentals is a little like the movie "The Secret Garden." You never know what you'll find on the other side of the fence—blight or beauty. Some tenants really do have a green thumb. Others just say they do. Tenants want a lawn, but they don't want to mow. They want plants, but they forget to water. They want a garden, but they run the water all night producing the $10 tomato. When the thrill of tending the garden is over, they leave you with weed-infested dirt mounds in place of a once green lawn. They want sidewalks, fences, planters and cute little flowers, but they have a dog that wets and a child who neglects the poop patrol. They want to dig a big fire pit, which becomes a pit fall for the next tenant.

I once spent two months in the heat of summer carefully watering and restoring the lawn at a rental house. A few months after the tenant moved in, I wondered why I had bothered. The once lovely yard looked like a moonscape, with only a few shreds of grass left. It was reduced to bare earth and littered with doggie dug craters, children's broken toys, trash and dog poop. You've heard of the two-hankie movie?…Well, this yard remnant rated three hankies, and the tears were on me.

Landscaping that Moves with the Tenant

Our apartment building had a nice little rose garden outside. To keep it looking good, I personally pruned and fertilized the roses each year. Miss Dusty Rose, a flamboyant tenant, especially liked to pick the roses and display them in her apartment. Miss Dusty Rose loved those roses so much that when she moved out, she had her boyfriend come over under cover of night to dig out her favorite rose bushes for transport to her new digs. Imagine my surprise to find, not roses, but gaping holes.

One tenant took a strong dislike to a huge ash tree standing in the frond yard, which shaded the house. Mr. Tree-Hater didn't like the fallen leaves or the space it took up in the front yard. He wanted it removed. This beautiful tree was 25 feet tall and had a trunk a good two and a half feet across. It added greatly to the beauty and value of the property.

We said "no way" to any chain sawing of the tree. Due to personal problems, Mr. Tree-Hater soon stopped paying the rent and we went though a long eviction process. In the midst of this, the lovely old tree went into decline and actually died. Now we had to take it down. When the tree-trimmer came to do the job, he called me over. Pointing out several good sized bore holes drilled into the trunk of the tree, he said, "This tree was poisoned!" It seemed that Mr. Tree-Hater had left us owing over $4000 in rent and had killed a beautiful tree for spite. Not everybody loves a tree.

Pruning Mania

Some tenant's idea of improving the landscaping is to prune 'til the landlord swoons. One tenant moved into a house with a lovely yard of healthy trees and shrubs as well as blooming rosebushes. Within a few weeks Mr. Pruning Shears had reduced everything to barren nubs. Since it was not the time of year for pruning, and the pruning was so extreme, most of the landscaping never recovered. We had to have the bare skeletons removed and replaced. Maybe we should go with a dessert theme next time—rocks and cactus.

While we were on vacation, Lumberjack Pete took it upon himself to remove a beautiful tree that the plumber told him was putting roots into the water line. Pete billed us for the 40 hours it took him to hack and saw our ten-year-old shade tree into a pile of limbs and sawdust. Thanks a lot.

Watering

Watering is another issue dripping with drama. Miss Penny Pinching broke up with her boyfriend and gave us a 30-day notice in the middle of summer when the heat spiked at over 100 degrees. When we took possession, we were shocked to find the lawns, small trees and most of the plants dead. Penny seemed surprised by our reaction. Didn't we know that she was strapped for funds? Not watering the lawns and shrubs had saved her a lot of money. Penny also made off with all the garden hoses and sprinklers, which we had supplied for her use. Maybe she planned to actually water at the next place.

The Responsible Landscape Lover

Some tenants do take pride in the yard. He will water and mow, mulch and fertilize. He asks for permission to plant flowers and a few new shrubs. A tenant with a green thumb can greatly improve the landscaping of your rental.

One conscientious college student made time every Saturday to mow the lawns at the house he and his roomies rented near the campus. When he stayed home sick one Tuesday morning, he was surprised to see a gardening crew arrive, rake a few leaves and get back into the truck. His landlord had neglected to inform him that the rent included the services of a gardener. The gardener seemed only too happy to get paid for not mowing the lawns.

Getting It Right

Landscaping adds to the beauty and value of your property. It also adds to your water bill. It is customary for the landlord to pay both trash and water. This is because you want to be sure that the trash gets hauled away and that your landscaping stays alive. Both contribute to the appearance of your property.

Go Over the Rental Agreement

Before singing the rental contract, go over the whole rental agreement with your tenant. This includes the **Yard Maintenance** portion. When it comes to landscaping, an ounce of prevention is worth a pound of cure. Since landscaping is an expensive and living part of your rental property, it needs special care. Neglect in this area by a tenant can cause your rental to look abandoned or trashed in short order. In a worse case scenario, a tenant who doesn't bother to water can cause you to lose all your landscaping including large trees and shrubs. So let your tenant know up front exactly what you expect, and what he can and cannot do with the existing landscaping.

Watering

You can encourage outdoor watering by installing lawn sprinkler systems and easy-to-use drip irrigation systems for the plants and trees. If a tenant has to move a sprinkler around the lawn, it is less likely to get watered than if he just needs to turn on a valve. Drip irrigation in the planting beds also makes watering a one step process. Drippers also use less water. Provide everything needed for watering the yard: hoses, sprinklers, nozzles, and easily accessible faucets. Note that you supplied these items on your Tenant Move-In Checklist.* These items are often ones that move when the tenant moves, and replacing them can be costly.

Since you are paying for the water, the tenant is more likely to water enough to keep the landscaping alive. It pays to check from time to time to see if the landscaping is being watered. If not, you can talk to the tenant about it, and encourage him to water more often.

The only thing worse that a tenant who doesn't water enough is one who over-waters. Since you are paying the water bill, he decides to run the sprinklers all night. Or he plants a huge garden, which he waters thoroughly every day. To head off this problem, I inform the tenant up front that I expect him to conserve water. If the water bill gets too high, I will call him and discuss the issue. This area is covered in the section of the rental agreement at the start of this chapter, which I go over with each tenant before the contract is signed.

Easy-Care Landscaping

Besides having an easy watering system, you want to have plants that can take a little neglect. Buy hardy, drought-tolerant plants. Something that has to be watered every 3-4 days in the heat of summer is likely to die. Perennials are better than annuals, which will have to be replanted each year. Choose trees that don't shed a lot of leaves or drop fruit on the sidewalk. Easy maintenance is the byword. Don't use poisonous plants like oleander or holly. Pets or kids might eat the leaves or berries.

Who Will Mow?

Getting the tenant to mow the lawns is another issue. Do they have a lawn mower? If not, are you willing to provide and maintain a lawnmower at this property? How often will they mow the lawn? What will they do with the lawn trimmings? What will you do if the lawns don't get mowed often enough to keep a neat appearance or at all?

If you do decide to let the tenant take charge of lawn mowing, you need to monitor it a bit especially at first. If the tenant is not mowing the lawns as agreed to, you can write him a letter reminding him of your agreement. *(You are to mow the lawn every 1-2 weeks depending on the growing season.)* In this letter you can tell him that if he doesn't comply with these standards, you will hire a gardener to mow the lawns and increase his rent to cover this added expense. You will need to give a 30-day notice to legally do such a rent increase.

Consider Hiring a Gardener

It may pay to hire a gardener to mow the lawns and add this expense to the cost of your rent up front. This way you know that the lawns will be mowed on a regular basis. They will be edged and kept up to a certain standard. With a gardener, you can also stay in charge of how much pruning is done and when.

A gardener can be your ally in seeing that the yard is being watered. He will be on the property on a regular basis to do the lawns and can report to you if he sees a problem.

Stay in Charge of the Yard

Never give a tenant a carte blanche to redo the yard. Otherwise you may find a tree planted within a few feet of the house, or the rose garden removed to make way for a hot tub, which will be gone when the tenant leaves. You will be stuck with the messy fruit tree, the root-cracked sidewalk, the tall bush planted in front of the window, or the paved-over former front lawn/basketball court long after the tenant is gone. Stay in charge of what is planted or removed from the yard of your rental. Make sure it is something you want for the long run.

You Can't Take it With You

Be clear about the fate of the landscaping upon move out. Anything planted in the ground on the property stays. If a tenant wants to take a plant with him, he should plant it in a pot. A tenant will often take out an existing planting to put in something different. However, he doesn't save this removed bush or tree for your later use. If each tenant is allowed to dig out everything he has planted over the years of his tenancy, whether you have paid for it or not, it will leave you with a bare yard and deep holes in your planters and in your pocketbook. So don't allow a tenant to remove the landscaping along with his possessions.

Gardens

Gardens are another hot-button item. Some tenants with visions of ripe-plum tomatoes dancing in their heads will want to rip out the lawn and plant a garden. The gardening bug is usually short-lived. The weeds and the tomato worms quickly replace the dream of zucchini bread. Don't sacrifice any good landscaping for the sake of a garden. When the season is over, you will be left with a weed infested dirt patch. Only allow a garden if there is bare ground that lends itself to that use. If you agree to a garden, first talk about water. A garden can use up a lot of water and can drive an otherwise mild water bill into triple digits if your water company has a graduated scale of use and payment rates. This is where the $10 tomato and the $5 zucchini come in. Insist that the would-be gardener install dripper irrigation, which cuts down on the amount of water needed. Set a cap on the water bill amount that you are willing to pay to accommodate the garden, say $10 a month over their usual water bill for that month. Have your tenant agree to pay the difference. You are unlikely to taste any of this produce, so use caution when approving a garden.

Be clear on your expectations for yard maintenance and check from time to time to be sure the yard is being watered and kept up.

Landscaping Checklist

- ❑ Go over the **Yard Maintenance** portion of rental agreement with the tenant.
- ❑ Encourage watering by installing sprinkling systems and drip irrigation.
- ❑ Discourage over-watering.
- ❑ Use hardy plants.
- ❑ Determine how often a tenant will mow the grass.
- ❑ Consider hiring a gardener.
- ❑ Stay in charge of the landscaping.
- ❑ Don't allow a tenant to take in-ground plants with him when he moves out.
- ❑ Be careful about allowing a garden.

You are the Landlord…Frisk future tenants for axes and pruning shears and remember the grass is always greenest over the septic tank.

This form is found at the back of this book.

Chapter 10

Improvements/Repairs

Repairs:

The Tenant shall do no repairs, decorating or alterations without the Owner's prior written or verbal consent. The Tenant shall notify the Owner in writing of any repairs or alterations contemplated and receive approval before the changes are made. Decorations include, but are not limited to: painting, wallpapering, hanging of posters or pictures; installing shelves, cabinets, or hooks that attach to the wall; replacing or removing fixtures, curtains, carpeting, or mini-blinds; removing or planting any shrubbery or trees on the property. A limited number of pictures (1-3 pictures per wall) may be hung with small nails on the walls providing all the nails are removed upon move-out.

The Tenant shall hold the Owner harmless as to any mechanics lien recordation or proceeding caused by the Tenant.

The Tenant shall keep the premises and furniture, furnishing and appliances (if any) and fixtures, which are rented for the Tenant's exclusive use in good working order and condition. The Tenant will keep the plumbing in good working order by not flushing items that will clog or impair the lines or septic system. .

The Tenant shall pay the Owner for the costs to repair, replace or rebuild any portion of the premises damaged by the Tenant, the Tenant's guests or invitees.

The Tenant's personal property is not insured by the Owner.*

This section is from the **Rental Agreement and the **Addendum to the Rental Agreement***

Improvements/Repairs: Beauty is in the Eye of the Beholder

As a landlord you are responsible for maintaining a nice home for somebody else. From time to time you may also want to improve the property for your tenant's benefit and to make the rental more desirable. When the roof is leaking, a faucet is dripping and the tenant asks if you'll replace the carpeting—it's a real juggling act to keep the rental functional, add some upgrades, and still break even.

The tenant rightly assumes that you'll take care of any repair problems right away. But he may have no idea of how expensive even simple repairs can be. In addition, most tenants can envision some improvements that would make their little home a lot nicer. The problem is that you as the landlord are asked to pay for these improvements. Some tenants never seem to understand that improvements cost money. Unless you raise the rent, the money is coming from directly from your pocket. It never occurs to some of your more pushy tenants that the carpeting in your own home may be older that theirs, but that you just take better care of it.

The following areas will test your patience and your pocketbook:

Carpeting

Carpeting is the bug-a-boo of rental maintenance. It is the first area to show signs of use and misuse. I have learned that most tenants just don't take care of their carpeting like you do. In your home you may be careful to eat in the kitchen/dining area, which has vinyl flooring. Your tenants and their children however, seem to live in front of the TV set in the living room or bedroom. This creates a nasty trail of food spills from the kitchen across the carpeting throughout the house.

Besides food and drink spills, some treacherous materials I have attempted to pry from the rental carpeting are candle wax, chewing gum, paint, nail polish, and super glue. These items defy the powerful chemicals of carpet cleaning and might mean a costly replacement. Cigarette burns are another fatal flaw inflicted on rental carpeting.

Picky Patty, a persistent tenant with an aversion to vacuuming, begged for new carpeting. Her carpeting was not all that old, but was looking the worse for wear due in large part to the energies of her two toddlers and her feisty pit bulldog. I finally relented and agreed to replace the carpeting. *"You won't be putting in used carpeting will you?"* Patty asked. I assured her that we always put in new good quality carpeting. After selecting two durable samples that were mid-range in price, I allowed her to go to the carpet center and decide which of the two she wanted. *"Is this all the choice I get?"* Mrs. Picky complained. I wondered if she realized that the new carpet would already cost nearly two full months of rent.

As fate would have it, the carpet installers came on a day that it drizzled. Patty's bed and some furniture had been moved outside and I quickly arrived to cover them with tarps. The installers found a weak board in the floor of a closet and pulled off the job until the flooring could be repaired. My husband spent several hours on his knees in the closet cutting and replacing the board. His reward? Mrs. Picky put her hands on her hips and noted in all seriousness, *"I think you should pay me something for all this inconvenience!"* Yeah, right.

Think that was nervy? Listen to this. One tenant decided that tenant rights extended to using the rental carpeting to improve his truck. He cut a large rectangle of carpet from the entryway of his apartment and used it to line his truck bed. After all he was moving soon.

Paint

When selecting a paint color (or allowing the tenant to do so) consider both taste and turnover. What is beauty to your present tenant may be bothersome or downright repugnant to the next one. For example, you just had the apartment painted in a neutral shade. The new tenant asks to repaint the small bedroom in pink and lavender for his young daughter. This not only challenges the third law of painting thermonuclear-dynamics (how may coats of paint can a wall actually hold before it implodes?), but the next tenant will most likely hate pink walls. He might have all boys or will want to use said room for a sedate office. If you allow a pink paint-over, you can bet that the departing tenant will not repaint back to the original neutral color before leaving, nor will he remove the glitter stars from the ceiling.

Tenants with an itch to use a paintbrush usually also lack credentials as professional painters. This means that light switches are likely to be painted over as is the molding, knobs, light fixtures and some of the carpet around the edges.

One tenant with questionable artistic talent painted a dark green drapery mural around the living room picture window. It took three coats of paint to cover it over when she moved out.

Plumbing

Plumbing is another issue that can bring out the worst in your tenant. And nothing sets your nerves on edge like an irate phone call from a tenant whose toilet has just overflowed. *"I'm not taking this shit,"* screamed Mrs. Fastidious early one morning over the phone. *"I'm missing a day of work because of the plumbing, and I'm standing in ____ and I can't deal with it!!! This is unsanitary and the Health Department won't like it!!"* The clogged plumbing was most likely the fault of what she and her three children had flushed lately, but I refrained from pointing that out. As the landlord, the shit stops with you. If your tenant has only a passing acquaintance with a plunger, buy her one and get a good pair of industrial strength plastic gloves for yourself.

Plumbing problems are a true emergency that is likely to set everyone on edge. Hugo, an upstairs tenant, was enjoying a nice morning shower when the apartment pipes began to back up. I got a frantic call from Wanda, a downstairs tenant, who noted with some alarm that brackish water was rising in her tub. I tried phoning Hugo who was still enjoying his hot shower, oblivious to the concerns below. No answer. Wanda's tub was fast nearing the overflow stage and her bathroom sink was gurgling in distress as well. I drove over and pounded on Hugo's door. A miffed, damp Hugo, wrapped in a bath towel with shampoo lather still in his hair emerged. He was in a bit of a lather himself. I now had two mad-as-a-wet-hen tenants. Ruffled feathers smell worse when sewage is involved.

Plumbing repairs are often needed for water, sewer or gas lines and their corresponding appliances. Utilities are a necessity no tenant likes to be without for long.

A tenant smelled gas at our six-unit apartment building and called the gas company whose representative shut off the gas to the whole complex. It took a plumber three days to dig out the lines, saw cut the sidewalk, replace all six lines (which were getting old) and reconnect everything. Then we had to pour a new replacement sidewalk. In the meantime the tenants were intermittently out of gas for their stoves, wall heaters and water heaters. Tempers were the only thing heating up.

A few weeks later the gas line to the laundry room began to leak as well. The same alert tenant put us through the identical drill. This time it involved saw cutting the entire width of the concrete driveway. While the ditch was open, we opted to replace the water line to the laundry room as a preventative measure. The driveway was a mess of noise, dirt, chunks of concrete and a gaggle of workmen. I probably should have notified all the tenants of the problem, but I thought that amid the mess, the repairs were rather obvious. During the excavation, a peeved tenant called to let us know that washer and dryer in the laundry room weren't working. Well yeah, I figured that.

Unexpected Repairs

Some repairs and maintenance are to be expected. Others come literally out of the blue.

One winter's night our town experienced a 70-mile per hour windstorm. The wind blasted in with surges that sounded like a freight train coming from a distance, then crashing with a roar against the house. I lay awake in the dark as the trees and bushes rattled and the wind roared. I knew I was in trouble when the phone rang at 4:00 am. A huge tree limb had come down on the roof of one of our rental houses, going completely through the roof (but fortunately not the ceiling) of a bedroom. Its fall had made a very large and terrifying sound and left a pretty large and terrifying hole. *"We could have been killed!"* shrieked Penny, the frightened tenant. I shared Penny's concern. It was a terrible night, and a terrible fright. However, there was not much I could do in the dark at four in the morning. *"I'm so sorry,"* I said. *"We'll take care of it as soon as we can tomorrow. I'm so glad no one was hurt!"*

At 7:00—at first light, I called the tree trimmer who, following the storm, was in great demand. While I waited for his return call, Penny phoned again. *"This is not a calm tenant calling….Why aren't you over here?"* she demanded. *"You don't know what I've been through. What are you going to do?"*

What I was going to do was to try and get a tree trimmer over there ASAP to get the tree limb off the roof. I didn't think I could lift if off with my bare hands. The tree trimmer soon arrived to remove the broken bough. Within the next few days, the roofer arrived to replace the roof. The carpenter arrived to replace the fascia board. And the painter arrived to paint the new fascia board. In the meantime I arrived to hold Penny's hand and reassure her that while the tree limb had fallen the sky was still there.

The same windstorm blew down two fences at different rentals. One was a 50-foot span, which required total replacement. Since you don't know which way the wind blows or what it will take with it, keep some ready cash in your stash at all times.

The Move to Improve

Repairs are a necessity. Improvements are discretionary. A clause in our rental agreement states that no improvements are to be made to the residence without the landlord's prior permission. This clause has not stopped tenants from painting, wall papering, hanging shelving with huge molly bolts, removing doors or putting hundreds of nails in a single wall. Such improvements rarely cause your property to be left in improved condition.

Miss Simplicity decided that she didn't want wall-to-wall carpeting in her apartment. So she simply ripped out all the carpeting to expose the hardwood floors beneath—a little improvement to her space. She had the nearly new carpeting hauled away. Never mind that I wanted carpeting in the apartment for a number of reasons and had paid considerable money to place it there. When Miss Simplicity moved, her security deposit was of course insufficient to cover replacing the carpeting, so her improvement was my added expense.

Mr. Halftime bought a new large-sized refrigerator. Unfortunately, it wouldn't fit through the doorway into the kitchen. No problem. Between innings he just ripped off the doorframes and rolled it right in. It wasn't until he moved out a few months later that I discovered the damage and paid the price for Mr. Halftime's new icebox.

Over the years I have grown suspicious of certain proposed improvements. Take fencing for instance. One concerned son called us about his elderly parents who were the tenants of a small house. It would be so nice, he proposed, to fence in the front yard for them so they would feel more secure. He won us over with his tender concern, and a nice little chain link fence went up. A few weeks later I noticed a small house trailer parked in back of the house and numerous children playing in the newly fenced front yard. The concerned son had moved himself, his wife, his three children, and a dog onto the property. He really did need that fence.

Mr. Eager Beaver had a week off from work while we were out of town. He informed us in his follow-up note, *"I didn't want to bother you, so I just did what I'd have wanted done if I were the landlord."* He installed a new range hood, painted over the brick in the kitchen, refinished the cabinets, hired a plumber, and took out a tree in the front yard that was supposedly growing roots into the drain line. Included with his note was a thick stack of bills including one for 60 hours of his own labor. Next time Mr. Eager Beaver has a few days off; I'd better take out a loan.

Beware of the tenant who says he is Mr. Fixit and who wants to exchange rent for work done on your rental house. You will usually get off cheaper and get a more professional job if you actually hire a professional and stay in charge of what you want done. Some of my worst carpentry jobs have been done by a Mr. Fixit who must have used a warped board for a straight edge. One Mr. Fixit actually worked as a finish carpenter. Because he had done some good carpentry work in my own home, I gave him the go ahead to replace his front door. I trusted in his professional judgment and he charged me a professional price as well. So I was more than a little surprised when he had installed a French door with glass panels all the way to the bottom—not exactly the secure dead-bolted front entrance I had envisioned. A short time later this Mr. Fixit broke his lease, bought the house next door, and left me with the his idea of an improvement.

Another tenant told us he had replaced the washers in his leaking faucet but said that the seat of the faucet was probably gone because the leak continued. My husband went to check it and found that it was not the washer but another part that had been mistakenly replaced. A set of twenty-cent washers stopped the drip, saved the day, and saved us the dire bill of a plumber house call for needless seat replacement.

Being a slow learner, I gave the go ahead for the friend of a tenant who had tiling experience to put a tile surround in the bathroom shower. We had talked about it and had agreed on white tile, white grout, and a reasonable price. Before the job was done, the price had doubled and the friend had gone with his buddy's idea and put in white tile with black grout. The tenant is long gone and we are still trying to learn to like black grout. It pays to hire a professional and stay in charge.

Getting it Right

Maintaining your rental property is no walk in the hardware store. It is a constant juggling act to balance your available finances with needed repairs and maintenance. Then you have to consider which improvements or upgrades (if any) you want to make. Here's where you start.

Step One—The Walkthrough

A good way to assess your rental is to have a checklist that you go through before renting the house or apartment, making sure everything is clean and in working order. Go through this **Walk-through Inspection Checklist*** as you survey the rental to decide what repairs are needed. If an area or an item is clean, is in working order, and has no damage, leaks or missing parts, you can just check the "**good**" **box** for that item. Otherwise, write down what is wrong with that item or area in the space next to it. This way you have a concise, room-by-room list of repairs needed.

Once the repairs are all done you will go over a fresh **Walk-Through Inspection Checklist*** with your new tenant prior to move in. Have him sign the list to verify that things are as represented. You can then go over the same checklist when the tenant moves out.

This will allow you to verify that any damage (broken windows, cracked tile etc.) that happened **after** the tenant moved in. Most vacating tenants are quick to say of any damage: *"It was like that when I moved in."* Rarely will a tenant admit that he broke a window, cracked the bathroom sink, or stained the carpeting.

If there is a damaged item, which you choose not to replace such as a cracked floor tile, be sure to list this on the inspection form. This relieves your tenant's mind that they might be blamed for the damage, and keeps you up to date on any damaged items that are not a new tenant's fault.

The value of the checklist is that it serves you better than your own memory or the honesty of some of your tenants. A **Walk-Through Inspection Checklist** is provided at the back of the book.

Before your tenant moves in, you need to make sure that everything is in good working order. Use your checklist to go over each room including the heater, air conditioner, stove, refrigerator, sinks, toilet, and bathtubs or showers, blinds, and outside watering systems. The walls should be clean and freshly painted or touched up with all holes patched. The carpet should be in reasonably good condition and professionally cleaned with no spots or damage. The windows should be clean with no cracks or broken windows. All windows should be able to be locked and have screens. The front door should have a deadbolt lock. For the security of you tenant, you will need to change the locks (have them re-keyed) for each new tenant. Even if the last tenant returned the keys, you do not know if he had any copies made that were not turned in.

Vinyl or tile flooring should be clean and well secured. The yard should be mowed and picked up with the landscaping in good shape. Any fences should be in good condition.

In addition to the walk-through inspection sheet, you need to keep a list of any major improvements made for each rental such as when you replaced the water heater, carpeting, stove, re-roofed a unit, etc. This way you can know how long an item has been in use, and have an idea of when a big item may need replacing.

Things will, of course, break down or need repair while your unit is rented. Ask the tenant to call you right away if something needs fixing. Don't put off needed repairs. Rentals house not only people, but also the volatile elements of water, gas and electricity. If something is questionable, fix it. Remember that an ounce of prevention is worth a pound of cure. Always make sure your rentals are safe.

Step Two—Doing the Repairs

If something is broken or not working, you need to fix it or replace it. I have found that it pays to buy good quality appliances, faucets, carpeting, paint etc. Tenants can be hard on these items and you will save money in the long run by buying products that hold up. This does not mean that you should buy top of the line, luxury appliances. A midrange well built appliance, faucet, or toilet is best.

Each landlord needs to decide which of these repairs he wants to do on his own and which ones he can afford to hire done. Unless you are extremely handy, you will need to develop a list of a reliable plumber, electrician, painter, roofer and general handyman. It is best to hire a professional to do any work involving electrical or gas hookups. A mistake here can be life threatening. Just a note—if you do a repair yourself, you can write off the materials, but not your own labor. If you hire something done, you can write off both labor and materials.

Finding Good Workmen

Finding good workmen at reasonable prices is like a treasure hunt. The good ones are gold. Once you find a good roofer, plumber or handyman, write his name and number in your address book in bold and stick with him. Be sure to praise his good work and pay him promptly. You may feel like kissing his feet. Why do I treasure a reliable repairman? Because I've had dealings with other not so reliable ones.

Time is money for your rental, so the workman who fails to show or the one who delays a repair job is not just an inconvenience, but a liability. I've had roofers who left the job half done while they went to the local watering hole, tree trimmers who've dropped a whole palm tree on the formerly fine fence, plumbers who pulled off the job leaving their tools but no message behind. Some plumbers use too small of a routing head on the plumber's snake, forging only a small hole in the blockage, thus insuring that they will need to return in a few weeks to do the job poorly again. Some large plumbing companies will insist that you need to pay over $1000 dollars to have them run a small camera down your lines to do a thorough and expensive check instead of just making the $200 repair.

I hired one painter who did a fine job of exterior painting. The only problem came when I gave him a partial payment him half way through the job. He took the money and never returned to finish the job. I've learned to pay only when the job is done.

Don't Shoot the Messenger

I was awakened from a sound sleep at 5:30 am by the shrill ringing of the phone. Iris, an elderly tenant at our apartment across town, was on the line. *"I've been up all night,"* she said. *"I smelled gas and had to try to sleep on the couch. I feel sick. And that new faucet you had put in yesterday to get rid of that leak…well, it's in but it's still leaking."*

I tried to clear my foggy brain to think. We'd just spent thousands of dollars at the apartment house replacing all of the gas lines. We'd had the plumber back twice to tighten the fittings. And the new faucet should have taken care of Iris's dripping one unless the new one was defective, or was not properly installed.

I didn't want to deal with any more problems. I didn't want to deal with Iris. I was sick and tired of the darn plumbing. Mostly I was just tired. I wanted to go back to sleep. I felt like shrieking—first at Iris and then at the incompetent plumber.

Fortunately, I was not wide-awake enough to go with my first impulse. Iris's words were beginning to sink in. *"Iris, take the phone outside. OK? Now take a few deep breaths. You're not smoking are you? No? OK, good. Stay outside now. We'll be right over."*

It was still dark when we pulled up at the apartment building. Iris's slim form, sitting on the stoop, was backlit from the yellow porch light. There was no gas smell at Iris's apartment. No gas smell at the new connections. All the pilot lights were lit. *"Well, maybe I just imagined it,"* said Iris. My husband removed a bit of gravel from the washer of the new faucet. The drip stopped. We called the gas company to do a check—just in case. We went home. Luckily I hadn't vented to Iris or to the hapless plumber. Sometime you just want to shoot the messenger.

Most often, the only time the tenant calls you is when there is a problem. The list of potential problems is endless. The toilet is backed up. The roof is leaking. Moisture is seeping in and bubbling a wall. Hot water is oozing out from under the water heater. There is a strange burning smell when the ceiling light is turned on. The trashcan has gone missing. The garbage disposal is stuck. A tree fell over in the back yard.

These calls can come at very inopportune times such as when you are frantically packing to go on a little vacation, or when you have just changed into your jammies for bed. Irritation and even anger on the part of the tenant can bring out the same in you. It's easy to blame the tenant for causing you the trouble and expense you know is ahead after getting his call. All he has to do is make a phone call. You have to take care of the problem.

In these moments it helps to take a few deep breaths and gain the calm to thank the tenant for letting you know of the problem. After all, it is your unit that will be flooded if the water heater trickle turns into a total burst of failure. It is your property, not to mention your tenant, that will be reduced to cinders if the electrical short turns into a fire. An alert tenant who informs you of a problem is doing you a favor…so don't shoot the messenger.

Plumbing

The most common maintenance issue is the plumbing. Decide on how you want your tenant to handle plumbing emergencies. I have the tenant call me and get an OK to call the plumber (one of my choosing). This way I can decide if I want to send my husband over to replace a washer, adjust a toilet valve, etc., or if this is a job better left to a professional. If a plumber is needed, I have found it works best to let the tenant make the call to the plumber so they can coordinate the time of the service call and be there to let the plumber in. Otherwise you are making calls back and forth as the middleman, and your might end up spending a lot of down time at your rentals waiting for the plumber. In an emergency, when I cannot be reached, the tenant knows which plumber to call.

Also, in the delicate area of plumbing, you will need to overcome any squeamishness about giving your tenant "the talk" when you go over the maintenance/potty portion your rental agreement. Especially if your rental is on septic, you need to discuss what can and cannot go down the toilet. No No's include feminine hygiene products, diapers, and condoms. These items can block the lines or float to the top of your septic tank and stop up your leech lines. While it is embarrassing to mention this up front to a relative stranger, it is even more embarrassing to have this talk with your tenant after the fact, in the presence of the septic tank pump-person who has the offending article(s) in hand. Keep a record of how often your septic tanks have been pumped. Every two years is a recommended time frame. Pumping on a schedule prevents leech line problems and expensive re-dos of the entire system. You also need to discuss what should not go into the garbage disposal. Ask your tenant to skip the watermelon rinds, eggshells and the coffee grounds. Spoons have a devastating effect on the disposal too.

Another plumbing tip. When faucets start leaking, have your plumber re-do the seats as well as the washers. Otherwise you will be calling often for washer replacement. It is cost effective to replace older faucets rather than continually trying to repair them. Plumbing house calls are expensive.

Electrical

Electrical problems are best handled by a professional. One of the calls I dread is the one that begins, *"When I turned on the light switch there was this flash of light and I smelled smoke!"* An electrical short is a fire waiting to happen, so take care of it fast. Sparky was a tenant who thought he could wire in a switch or a light on his own. I encouraged him to let me call a qualified electrician for any such contemplated improvements. One day he phoned with *"the light switch sparked/I smell smoke"* line. I dispatched an electrician over there pronto. It seems that Sparky had placed two 250-watt bulbs in the light fixture, which was rated for only two 60-watt bulbs. The 500 watts of energy surging through had fried the wiring. The wall switch had also been rewired improperly. I can only hope Sparky has leaned not to play with fire or the wiring.

Carpeting and Flooring

Carpets and flooring take the most wear and tear of any item in your rental. A brand new carpet or vinyl floor can be ruined by a careless tenant in short order. Find out the name of a good carpet cleaner and a reasonable carpet and flooring outlet. Your carpet at home may last 10 years, but a rental carpet has an underfoot life of about four years. Buy a good quality professional grade carpet in a neutral shade that will go with any tenant's furnishings. Anything too light or too white is doomed. Tile might seem like a good alternative to vinyl flooring, which is easily damaged, but a cracked or chipped tile is no easy fix either. Tile can last a lot longer, but it is a lot more expensive to install and to replace if damaged.

Appliances

Most rentals include a stove, heating and (depending on the climate) air conditioning. I usually do not include a refrigerator in my rentals. Most tenants have their own refrigerator, which they want to use. If your unit has a refrigerator and the new tenant has one also, you will have to move and store a refrigerator. Refrigerators are very heavy and unwieldy. You'd have to be built like a hefty football player to get a fridge safely up and down stairs. It is also dangerous to store a refrigerator due to the possibility of a small child crawling inside, closing the door, and suffocating. This is a liability you don't need. It is also no picnic cleaning a refrigerator once it has been left unplugged by your last tenant. So, in most cases, let the tenant supply the refrigerator.

Other appliances that I do not usually supply are a washer/dryer or a microwave. These are appliances that the tenant can easily provide and any appliance with your name on it is one you have to maintain repair, replace and clean when the tenant leaves.

Fixtures

Fixtures and other items that you will need to maintain are sink, tubs, showers, toilets, lights, fans, medicine cabinets, towel racks, countertops, doors, windows, screens, garage doors, and window coverings like mini-blinds and curtains. If you want to upgrade a unit, a new sink or toilet can be a nice improvement. Tile countertops that look dirty can be re-grouted if the tile is in good condition. Mini blinds or vertical blinds seem especially to take a beating, so I make sure to note their condition upon move in. You cannot easily replace one missing vertical blind or a crumpled bottom set of slats on a mini-blind, so any damage usually means total replacement.

The Reserve Account

This brings us to the necessity of the reserve account. When repairs are needed, they cannot and should not be put off. Therefore you need to have money on hand to meet these little and big emergencies. Replacing carpeting or a major appliance can eat up several months of rent. A leaking roof is a major expense to replace. As a landlord, you cannot afford to live on the edge financially. Others are counting on you for the security of their home/your rental. When a plumbing, sewer, electrical or gas leak problem arises, your tenant's well being is at stake.

If you have more than one rental, it is even more crucial to keep money in reserve for the unexpected. A flooded apartment, an unexpected move out, or an air-conditioner burnout in August, can all demand immediate financial CPR. It is your responsibility as a landlord to keep things in good working order and to be sure that there are no safety or sanitary issues. Being a slumlord is not for you. Keep money in reserve earmarked for rental use only. I recommend a reserve amount of at least $1000 per rental unit. It is a necessity to have an emergency fund for those unexpected winds of life.

Improvements

Every tenant can think of improvements they think will make their place a little nicer. Who wouldn't like new carpeting, a covered patio, a new stove, or new cabinets in the kitchen? Some tenants can be very pushy when asking for or demanding changes or additions to their cozy abode.

Your challenge as a landlord, is to balance improvements and your checkbook. You want to keep your rentals up to a certain standard. You don't want to devolve into a slumlord or let you rental fall into disrepair. That said, you are **not** Santa Claus. You cannot make every tenant's wish list come true on the amount of rent they are paying. Every improvement costs money. At times you may feel that a certain rental needs a total makeover. This may eat up your profits for several years but give you a more marketable unit down the road. If you never put money into improving your rentals they eventually will fall into ruin. On the other hand, how often can you afford to totally replace the carpeting or buy a new stove? While you can raise the rent a bit to cover upgrades between tenants, an existing tenant rarely wants to pay more rent in exchange for new carpet.

So, stay in charge of any improvements you make in your rentals. If the carpet needs replacing, replace it. If a tenant wants a luxury item, think about it. You can and often should say no. Can you really afford to put up a covered patio at your rental house, or should you spend your money on putting in a new septic system at your older unit?

Tenants by nature are temporary residents in your units. The average stay for a tenant, depending on the area, is 6 months to 2 years. What is a fashion statement for one tenant may be a drawback for the next. Keep colors neutral and wallpaper off the walls. Don't allow any big mounting bolt to make holes in the walls. Don't let the tenant remove the lawn and dig a deep and wide hole for a doughboy pool in the backyard. Think in terms of what your house will look like when the tenant leaves and takes part of the improvement with him—like the shelving but not the screw-holes in the paneling: the pool, but not the hole in the backyard. Don't count on him to replace the grass or repair the holes in the walls or in the yard. Will the next tenant really want purple carpeting, a painted medallion on the concrete patio, or a cactus garden by the back door?

You are the one who will have to pay for the improvement and live with it down the road long after the tenant is gone. Does it fit into your overall plan for the rental? Is it something that will make the unit more desirable to future tenants? Can you afford it at this time?

Rental Repairs Checklist

- ❏ Do a walkthrough of the rental with the **Walk-Through Inspection CheckList** * to assess repairs needed.
- ❏ Make any needed repairs.
- ❏ Go over a new **Walk-Through Inspection Checklist*** with the new tenant prior to move in.
- ❏ Keep a list dating major improvements and appliance purchases for each rental.
- ❏ Keep rental and appliances in good repair.
- ❏ Don't shoot the messenger.
- ❏ Have a plan with the tenant for plumbing emergencies.

❑ Fix any electrical or plumbing problems promptly.

❑ Provide only a minimum of appliances.

❑ Keep a reserve account to fund emergency repairs.

❑ Agree only to improvements you really want and can afford to do.

Keeping your rental in good condition is a challenge, but it pays off in fewer emergency calls, a happier tenant, the long-term condition of your rental, and in attracting a better tenant.

You are the Landlord...keep that plunger handy.

This form can be found at the back of this book.

Chapter 11

Rental Uses

*This rental is intended for residential use only. The Tenant may **not** use this rental property at any time to conduct any type of commercial business. This includes, but is not limited to: babysitting, child-care, car repairs, lessons, book-keeping, consignment projects, massage, or any business which requires customers to come onto the property. Our liability insurance does not cover such ventures. Any use of this property for such a business would be considered a breach of the Rental Agreement.**

This portion is from the **Addendum to the Rental Agreement*

A Little Business on the Side

The above clause was added to our Addendum after we discovered that some tenants could be really creative in using and sometimes abusing your property. For a few tenants, it is not enough that your rental provides their housing. A really ingenious one can figure out how your unit can also help provide his livelihood or a little extra income on the side.

Over the years our rentals have been used as a base for all of the following: a child day care center, a massage parlor, a karate studio, a woodworking shop, a spray paint artist studio, an auto repair garage, a computer marketing business, a publication central office, a methamphetamine lab, a drug sales area, and a house of prostitution.

Each of these endeavors carries a varying degree of desirability and liability for your property.

Childcare

Childcare or varying degrees of babysitting is a moneymaking business that a stay-at-home-mom or even a grandma may hope to add to your property. She might be blissfully unaware of your extreme liability in having a passel of toddlers on your property. And she can be equally unconcerned about the state of your septic system, not to mention the complaints of the other tenants to whom you promised a nice quiet area.

Misty lived in a rental house a block away from the neighborhood elementary school. After the second unexpected pumping of the septic tank, which mysteriously filled at an alarming rate, overflowing into the yard, we discovered that she had a nice little after school daycare business going. A dozen kids and a few assorted dogs gathered there each day after school for snacks and recreation. The septic system, which was workable for Misty's family of five, was overtaxed by the needs of her little business on the side. While money was flowing into Misty's pocket, it was gushing out of ours, trying to keep up with the sewage.

Your expectations may not be the same as those of our tenant. Unless you spell it out up front, you may find out that a lot of unexpected guests are on your property.

Flo, other wise know as Nanny, was a grandmother of six. We didn't know this until after we had rented a small house to her and her husband. Neither did we know that Nanny baby-sat all of her grandchildren on a regular basis along with a passel other neighborhood children. The neat little rental house soon looked like an illustration for *"There was an Old Woman Who Lived in a Shoe—had so many children she didn't know what to do."* Only in this case it was the landlord who wasn't sure what to do. Kids clambered out of windows. Toys littered the tufts of green amid the bare dirt that formerly was the lawn. Limbs were ripped off of the trees and used for clubs. The picket fence was pilfered for fort building. Instead of the expected low wear and tear from an elderly couple, we got excessive wear and total tearing around. Inside was a wreckage of unmade beds, crushed crackers and chewing gum ground into the carpet, crayon on the walls, a ring around the tub and nothing rosy to report. Nanny's grandmotherly instincts and fixed income were nicely supplemented by this arrangement. We were just **in** a fix. In our naiveté we had even given Nanny and her husband a break on the rent, as it would just be the two of them. Either Nanny couldn't count or she believed that miscellaneous children didn't count.

Customer Service

Besides babysitting, any other business that can be run out of a home or in the yard thereof can creep into your rental, usually without your knowledge or permission.

Tenants have opened their doors to customers who came in to receive massage, karate lessons, assorted drug purchases, and prostitution services.

I wondered why Sasha had so many visitors. Cars came at regular intervals parked for 45 minutes and then left. Sasha's mailbox soon sported an added listing for the HiLo Dojo. Her customers were coming into our triplex to learn karate kicks, accompanied by loud intimidating yells. When it came to Sasha's new business, I had to do a little kicking and yelling of my own.

Lola was a massage therapist. I neglected to ask her up front where she worked. As it turned out, Lola worked in the den of our rental house where her massage oils took a decided toll on the carpeting. Her many clients and their parked cars also took a toll on the peace of the neighboring tenants. By the time the use of the property issues were all straightened out, I could have used a massage myself.

The Home Office

Even when the little business on the side doesn't bring customers unto your property it can bring in other undesirable elements like delivery trucks, extended phone lines, and employees with their parked cars.

With the advent of the E-business many people can work from home. This can work out fine until the simple home office begins to feel like a business district.

Sid moved into a triplex located close to our home. We thought we were getting a quiet single person until Sid turned a small alcove in his two-bedroom unit into a computer station for three employees. It seemed that Sid published a weekly newsletter and figured he could do it all quite cost effectively from the security of his rental. Before we could react, the phone company arrived to install extra phone lines. The UPS truck began to roar in and out of our driveway to make a daily run for our tenant's pickup and deliveries. Our trashcans filled with copious amounts of discarded business paper and used cardboard boxes. Employees began to arrive to fire up the computers, mail the invoices, and take up the parking spaces designated for our actual tenants. Sid's workers lunched on the table on the front lawn, had pizza delivered, and added to our septic problems. Sid's business meant that we were getting the business. A home business that gets too big makes a booming business district out of your nice quiet rental.

Setting Up Shop

Creative tenants can see possibilities everywhere. Frank, an elderly tenant, quietly took over the small storage space by the carports at our apartment building to start up a little woodworking business. He made birdhouses and wooden toys that he sold on weekends at flea markets. During the week, the screech of his electric saws and loud hammering was enough drive his neighboring tenants crazy. The sawdust from his projects flew over the short separating wall of the carport and onto the tops of the other tenant's parked cars. Most people only need scrapers for snow. Frank's carport mates needed scrapers to daily clear their windshields of a layer of sawdust before heading out. Frank was unconcerned. As a plus for his carpentry shop, he knew that the electricity in the carport area was on us. Because he was elderly and this was his hobby/business, we tried to bear with him, as did his longsuffering neighbors. Our payoff came when Frank moved out, leaving behind a storage room covered with two feet of sawdust and assorted piles of wood scraps. He took his tools and all the cute birdhouses with him.

After Frank's tenancy we shoveled out all the wreckage, put a new garage on the storeroom and made a deal with another tenant who had an antique store in town. He was willing to give up his carport space to use the now-locked storeroom for some of his antiques. This was a win/win situation with a tenant's business and our space. Antiques are pretty quiet and just gather dust instead of creating it.

Vehicle repair can be another troublesome business on the side. One tenant brought cars onto the property for his car-repair business. His driveway had plenty of space to accommodate two or three cars in various stages of distress. So what if a little oil leaked onto the cement or if the air gun was a bit strident. He saved a bundle in licensing and garage rental fees.

Another tenant was a talented artist. Emilio was especially good with an airbrush. This talent seem to be a plus until a huge bus pulled onto our property. It seems that Emilio had taken on the job of painting the sides of the tour bus for a rock group. The roar of the compressor, smell of paint and bulk of the bus added little to the ambience of the country house he rented from us. His neighboring tenants especially objected to the spotlight he cranked on to allow him to paint at night when inspiration was at it's highest. Emilio inspired me too. I was inspired to add one more addendum to my little rental agreement and one more experience to my landlord belt.

Monkey Business

Even animals can become a little side business. Tenants can raise rabbits, dogs, birds, goats, exotic animals, or even horses on your property. In these cases the manure is often the doer-in of this arrangement. Where does it go and who has to smell it in the meantime?

If you have a corral on your property it is an invitation for creative and not so creative bargaining and shuffling for possession. Remember the cowbird who takes over the nest of a lesser bird by shoving out the existing babies? I became the lesser bird.

Gladys move into a triplex on our property and promptly asked about adding her horse to our corral. I wasn't too eager to comply as we had our own young Arab gelding in there already. It wouldn't be easy to keep the alfalfa or the feedings separate, and who would clean up the manure from two horses? Gladys was paying big boarding fees elsewhere and saw our corral as a chance for free room and board for her mare. Gladys wouldn't take no for an answer. One day while I was away, she took the opportunity to move her horse into our corral. He was the dominant animal and a huge kicking match broke out. When I returned home, my horse was sporting a horseshoe shaped wound on his rear. She saved on boarding fees, but we had to consult a vet.

Charlie raised racing pigeons in a large coop he had built in the side yard of the house he rented from us. He seemed to keep the area clean and the pigeons were not loud or annoying. Charlie traveled on weekends to special meets where the pigeons were released to find their way home in record time. When Charlie and his wife divorced after several years in our rental, he gave us notice. What I had not expected was that before he moved, Charlie had to kill all of his prize pigeons. Our rental was home to these birds and they could not be retrained to return anywhere else.

Subletting

The most objectionable business on the side is when a tenant decides make money by renting out **your** property. Maybe he wants to go on an extended vacation, and thinks he'll move someone else in to cover the rent. Or perhaps he wants to rent out a room to make ends meet. Maybe he thinks he can get more for the apartment than he is paying you. Your tenant is <u>not</u> the landlord—at least not for your property. Dispel up front any myths he might have in this area with a good **Rental Agreement*** and **Addendum*** that clearly says, "No Subletting." See Chapter 4 on the Rental Agreement for more on subletting.

Getting It Right

Most tenants are content to just have a nice place to live. They have jobs elsewhere that serve to pay the rent. But occasionally a tenant is eyeing your rental as a site to do business. How can you head off the problems of a little business on the side in your rental?

Decide What You Want

Decide ahead of time what you want and do not want for your rental. Remember that any business that requires people other than your tenants to come onto the property may cause some liability issues for you. What if a child coming there for childcare is injured playing in the backyard? What if a massage customer feels he was injured by the massage therapist in your rental or trips and falls on the way out? Does your liability insurance cover such scenarios? Do they carry workman's compensation insurance for the do-it-yourself auto mechanic or carpenter injured on your property? Probably not.

It is OK to refuse to let your rental be used for any type of business. You are not renting it out as a commercial business property, but as a home rental. This is the best use of your property for you as the landlord.

Check Your Liability

It is important to check your insurance policy before allowing any on site business in your rental. We carry fire insurance and liability insurance on all of our rentals. Most insurance policies of this type however, stipulate that your property is being used as a private residence, not a business. To have coverage for a business use such as childcare would most likely be an additional cost to you. In today's litigious society, you cannot afford to be careless in this area. The deep pockets might be yours.

Use Caution in Allowing any On-Site Business

I recommend not allowing any business on your property that requires customers to come onto the property. Traffic, wear and tear and liability are all issues that arise when people other than your tenants are coming onto a property on a regular basis.

Childcare, for example, creates a host of liability issues as well as a huge impact on your rental itself. Instead of your known tenants, childcare brings an unknown number of children and their parents onto your property. Children are hard on a yard and on the carpets. The neighbors are subjected to a lot of cars coming and going for drop off and pick up as well as the noise of many children playing. You will not be getting any benefits from this use of your property, only more repair expenses. The tenant making money on childcare is not paying you extra rent for this purpose, nor will he be paying for the faster wearing out of the carpets, paint, plumbing, and landscaping. You will.

I also recommend being very careful if you do allow any other sort of home based business. Consider the impact on your rental, your available parking and the impact on the neighbors. Do you really want your property used as a car repair center, a massage parlor, a karate studio or a storage yard? I think not.

Ask

When you are sizing up a prospective tenant, ask upfront, *"Do you plan on using this rental to conduct any type of business?"* Clarify with a few examples: *"Babysitting? Childcare? A home-based business? Massage?"* Ask this question when you are still in the talking stages before the rental agreement is signed. Then if the tenant says "yes," you can find out the particulars.

What does he mean by a home-based business? Will he have any one beside himself working in this business? Would it mean employees or customers coming onto the property? What changes would he have to make to your rental for this business? Extra phone lines? Special shelving? Additional cars? Extra trash? Air tools? A car lift?

Even if a prospective tenant says that he is not going to be conducting a business on the property, find out about the possibility of extended family babysitting. Be sure to ask if he/she will be taking care of any grandchildren, stepchildren or having any overnight visitors on a regular basis. Having extra relatives in the house might not qualify as a business, but you need to know how many people your rental is actually going to house on a daily basis. Even if the childcare is done for free, it impacts your rental. What you thought was a nice elderly couple can quickly become daycare central behind your back. The easiest way to stay in charge in this area is to ask.

Spell it Out

The best way to protect yourself and your rental from the vicissitudes of uses other than housing is to spell it out in your rental agreement. The clause at the beginning of this chapter was one I added to our rental agreement after getting stung by some unexpected abuses to our rentals. I make it clear to a tenant as they sign the agreement that any business venture run out of the rental that has not been OK'd by me is a breach of the rental agreement. The rental is for residential use only. Not for commercial business use.

Rental Uses Checklist

- ❑ Decide what you want for this rental. Will you allow any sort of business?
- ❑ Check your liability.
- ❑ Use extreme caution in OKing any business that brings others onto the property.
- ❑ Carefully consider the impact of any business venture to your rental.
- ❑ Ask the prospective tenant if he is planning to use the rental for any type of business.
- ❑ If the answer is yes, and you don't want to allow a business use, it is OK to refuse to rent to this tenant.
- ❑ Spell out what you want and don't want in your rental agreement.

You are the Landlord…Don't put up with any monkey business.

*This form is found at the back of this book.

Chapter 12

Feuds

The Resident will not violate any governmental law in the use of the premises, annoy, molest or interfere with any other resident or neighbor. *

This section is from the **Rental Agreement.*

Can't we all just get along?

Most tenants are wonderful people. They try hard to get along with others. In my 20 plus years of landlording, I have had problems with perhaps only 1 out of every 20 tenants. I want to remind you of this fact, because if you only look at the following stories, you might decide that becoming a landlord is a real Nightmare on Elm Street. I'm here to tell you that if you play it right, you can minimize the problems, and actually enjoy this very important business of providing nice housing for others. The stories are a cautionary tale of what can happen if you don't pay attention to the "Getting It Right" sections of this book.

While most tenants get on amazingly well with their neighbors, it is the few who don't who give you nightmares. Badly behaved tenants create problems for you, for their neighbors and for law enforcement. These are the tenants who have loud, out-of-control parties. Their guests park in the neighbor's parking space, and urinate on their lawns.

In extreme cases, some of these delinquent tenants progress from problem to felon by breaking the law in the use of your rental. He/she might sell drugs, solicit for prostitution, grow marijuana in the back yard, or produce methamphetamine in the kitchen sink. An argument may grow from angry words to destruction of the property to physical assault to murder. Which isn't exactly Mr. Rogers Neighborhood.

Fortunately, most tenant fusses and feuds will be of a much milder nature. Tenants will leave clothes in the communal washer, hang annoying wind chimes, place potted plants in the walkway, or block their neighbors view with a parked motor home. Spouses and lovers will quarrel, threaten, and separate. Children will skateboard in the driveway, do pull-ups on the community clotheslines, and stomp loudly while going up the stairs. Dogs will bark, neighbors narc or rat on each other and you will find yourself trying to keep the peace.

Lover's Quarrels

The most dangerous feuds to deal with happen within the walls of your rental between husband and wife or boyfriend and girlfriend.

One female tenant divorced and remarried while living in the same apartment. Her new husband Clyde told me that if his new wife's ex ever showed up he had plans to lure him inside and bump him off. I was pleased when they gave notice soon after with no blood actually spilled on the carpet.

Another time I was not so fortunate. This time a woman tenant actually murdered her husband in our rental house. Their volatile relationship ended in the kitchen. Mr. Unlucky in Love had three stab wounds and 112 puncture wounds in his back from a meat cleaver. Mrs. Unlucky's story in court was that her husband had accidentally fallen into the knife. Three times? Mrs. Unlucky went to prison, and I went from shock to denial, to dealing with the aftermath. It involves calling in hazardous waste specialists and hoping the next prospective tenant isn't superstitious. A murder in your rental is off-putting, to say the least, for you as well as for future tenants.

One couple moved in and the husband died suddenly and mysteriously soon after. I wanted to be sympathetic to the grieving widow, but found it difficult when she moved in a much younger boyfriend within the week. I still have my suspicions.

Another tenant went through a nasty divorce and soon moved in a boyfriend. They spent a night drinking, fighting and doing drugs and tore every door in the place off its hinges. The neighbors called the police who quieted things down temporarily. An eviction notice had a more lasting calming effect on the rental.

Rosy didn't put much stock in appearances. She had an on and off again relationship with her boyfriend, Rufus. After their latest breakup, Rosy hung a huge banner from the apartment balcony. It read, *"Go to Hell, Rufus!"*

When it comes to love and romance, you never know what might happen next. I once rented a small house to a single man. Mr. Loner assured me that he didn't need a roommate and was happy living alone. A few weeks later, he sheepishly admitted that his wife and young son, whose existence was previously unknown to me, had just come into the country and were now living with him. The wife had just signed the **Rental Agreement*** when the marriage went south in a hurry. Mrs. Loner quickly got a restraining order against her husband and kicked him out of the house. Soon all manner of different folks and assorted relatives were living in the house and our original tenant was forbidden by law from living there.

Squabbling Relatives

Next to feuds between husband and wives and assorted lovers, the fusses between relatives can be the most mean-spirited.

A grandmother lived in the downstairs apartment while her grandson and his bride rented the upstairs unit directly overhead. When Granny was a little too free with the advice, her grandson's wife showed her displeasure by doing a little tap dance on the ceiling above. Not to be outdone, Granny stepped outside, turned on the faucet and placed the gushing garden hose in the open window of her grandson's truck.

Two squabbling relatives once rented apartments at opposite ends of the building. They walked back and forth to deliver insults, went through each other's garbage, and monitored the arrival and departure times of any visitors. Each complained to me about their rival's activities. I fantasized about putting up a roll of razor wire fencing on the sidewalk out front to keep them apart.

Territorial Disputes

It has been said, *"Good fences make good Neighbors."* ("On Fences" by Robert Frost) Don't count on it. One rental property is a big lot with three houses. The large yard was once a communal property where the kids enjoyed games on the front lawn, played chase around the trees and used the swing-set together. The adults shared a bar-b-que and a sense of neighborliness. Then the feuds began. The back house had too many guests, who drank too much beer and kept the kids in the middle house up way past their bedtime. The husband of one house was accused of peeping into the window of another. The dog from the front house pooped on the front porch of the middle house. The kids weren't getting along. No one wanted to share.

In the early spring, fences began to sprout up faster than weeds. Territories were staked out and the view gave way to a slew of no trespassing signs. Now everyone has his own little space. But hidden behind their fences, this former Shangri La is not the open lawn of neighborliness it once was. *Something there is that just doesn't love a wall.* (Robert Frost)

Space is often an issue in feuds. Tenants can become very possessive of their space and any perceived trespassing thereof. This is my parking space…my view…my 26 inches of deck space…my day for the laundry room space.

Jungle Jane lived upstairs in an end unit—the one everyone else upstairs had to walk past on their way to and from the stairs. Jane started her landing landscaping with a few plants and a wind chime. Over time her little oasis grew to include potted trees, rocks, a table and chairs, sea shells, plaster animals, hanging plants, sculptures and a jungle of real and artificial flowers. When her tropical treasures reached to the door jam of the next unit, Jane started adding pots and colorful rocks to each of the stairs. When she watered, the overflow dripped through the landing and grew slippery moss on the front porch of the unit below. The jungle juice was also rotting out the decking. As you can imagine, dodging this plethora of philodendrons and hanging obstacles became a major annoyance and a safety hazard for her fellow tenants. Pruning back a jungle is a lot harder than nipping it in the bud with some tenant guidelines.

Space issues don't end at the property line. One tenant called to complain that a neighbor insisted on parking at the curb in front of his rental house under the shade of a large tree—his tree. There was plenty of on street parking space in front of the neighbor's own house, but no shade. No matter where the shade from your tree falls, the parking on the street is still public parking. So there is no law against the neighbor taking our tenant's favorite spot, other than the law of being a good neighbor and letting someone park in the shade of his own tree.

Noise Issues

Next to space, noise is the next most aggravating factor in just getting along. "I want a nice, quiet tenant," I told the single mom applying to rent a house located close to other residences. She assured me that she and her two very responsible and very quiet teenage daughters were perfect for our rental house. What she neglected to tell me was that she also had a troubled teenage son who knew all the other delinquent teenage boys in the neighborhood. Soon our property became party central. Loud music blared and underage drinking escalated as Mom was away at work each night. The neighbors put in the first of many calls to the police. A major fistfight on the front lawn was the final blow and the start of the eviction process. I really did want a nice quiet tenant.

When it comes to feuds, the closer the quarters, the louder the shoe falls. Tenants complain about people who tromp around too late at night, TVs and music that are played too loud, slammed doors, crying babies, and loud car mufflers that roar to life early in the morning. Most people think that noise is something someone else makes. But when it comes to fusses and feuds, noise is in the ear of the beholder.

One loudly quarrelling couple in an apartment raised the ire of their upstairs neighbor who called us the next morning to complain. Our answering machine recorded his series of calls. *"I can't take it anymore. I can't get any sleep!"* Beep…*"I tried to talk to the guy and he called me an SOB. I'm thinking of moving out. My nerves are shot!"* Beep…A few hours later…*"We finally had a heart to heart. I gave him a little marriage advice. Now we're like roomies. As of now there is no problem.!"* Was this a series of phone messages or an unfolding soap opera?

When the Beef's with You

Most feuds are between tenants or with their neighbors. Occasionally a feud gets more personal. That's when the tenant's beef is with you.

A tenant may not want resolution as much as he wants restitution for some real or imagined injury or breech of contract. It doesn't matter how nice of a landlord you think you are—sometime a tenant sees dollar signs and decides to sue you.

Lilly Lawsuit claimed that she had tripped and fallen down the defective back stairs of her apartment and severely injured her back. She somehow managed to have pictures of herself taken while she was sprawled at the bottom of the steps. The stairs were always kept in good repair. So I was surprised to see that after the "accident" one wooden step was pulled completely up from its moorings. Lilly made lots of visits to the doctor and collected from our insurance company. To be on the safe side we replaced all the wood stairs with cement ones. Years later her ex-husband admitted to us that he had helped Lilly pull up the step and defraud our insurance company and us. No kidding….

The tenant of a friend sued for supposed carbon monoxide poisoning from a defective wall heater. The heater was never shown to have any venting or other problems. There was no carbon monoxide buildup whatsoever in the apartment, but she claimed to have incurred permanent breathing problems. In a strange twist, the tenant also sued to stay in the offending apartment for an additional three months rent-free while the lawsuit was going on. If you really thought a heater was poisoning you, would you stay there a minute longer? The judge didn't buy it either. She lost the suit.

Getting it Right

OK. You're getting the idea that everyone may not just all get along. An eviction may ultimately be the only way to end some feuds. How can you keep fusses and feuds to a minimum?

Select Good Tenants

First of all, you can take your time and select good tenants. Select tenants who like to live a quiet lifestyle. Select tenants who have a track record of getting along with their neighbors. Check their references and if possible talk to their former neighbors. Find out if someone will be home to supervise children—especially teenagers. Ask to meet the children or teens to get an idea of their demeanor and behavior. See Chapter 3 for more details on Selecting the Tenant.

Choose Compatible Tenants

Try to find tenants with compatible life-styles when placing them near each other. A quiet apartment building is no place for a party animal. A couple with three rambunctious children might not do well next to an elderly couple. A tenant with three wandering cats won't mix well with the lady next door who has fur allergies. It's a little like the dating game without the bonus round. If you can put a similar mix of people together, they just might find the common ground to be friends.

Divide and Conquer

Fences and other dividing lines help keep the peace. As much as possible, create clear boundary lines indicating whose space is whose. If common yards surround a group of houses, delineate which portion goes with which house. For example at one triplex, the front lawn and nearby parking spot goes to the front apartment. The back lawn, carport and a shed go to the side apartment, and another unit gets a portion of back lawn separated by a tall hedge and a close in parking space. Each tenant is responsible for watering their portion of lawn, and has a private space to park and to sit outside. If possible, assign parking spots for each tenant whether in a carport or on the street. People like to have a routine place to park. Fighting for a parking spot is just one more aggravation. If a garage or carport is shared, you may even want to paint lines along the floor to delineate where one space stops and the other begins. People get very possessive about their space.

People also get possessive about their view. If possible, don't allow large motor homes, boats, or trailers to be parked where they will block a tenant's view. You can require that recreational vehicles be stored in a storage facility, not in front of someone's window.

A lot of feuding can be headed off by dividing the available space fairly among the tenants. A little fencing for visual separation, and assigning areas to each tenant can help ward off conflict. Any shared space leaves grounds for misuse, misunderstanding, and miscommunication.

Set Down Ground Rules

Good fences may not always make good neighbors, but good ground rules can help. You can head off certain problems by setting down guidelines for all of your tenants. Determine ahead of time which parking space belongs to which tenant. Define exactly which space goes with which house or apartment. Some rules for neatness can keep one person's stuff out of another person's space. We use our **Addendum*** to the **Rental Agreement*** to cover some of these space issues. For example, in the carports everything must fit into the locked storage lockers. Nothing else except the car and a bicycle can be stored in the carport. This includes boxes, mattresses, furniture etc. This keeps your carport area neat and keeps rats, cats and feuds over whose space is who's from taking over.

For our apartments, I have written guidelines in the **Addendum*** for what can and cannot go on the common porch areas. A doormat is OK. No wind-chimes, plants, tables, chairs, bicycles, or bar-b-ques allowed as these items blocks access for the others who have to walk by. I go over these guidelines with each tenants prior to move-in, so many problems never develop.

Guidelines can also help keep the peace in any shared area. If you have a Laundry Room, you can post Laundry room rules. This can include a sign-up sheet for reserving use times and instructions for such items as not leaving clothes unattended for long periods and cleaning the lint filter. Unattended lint cannot only start a fire, but a feud when the conscientious tenant always has to clean up after the tenant before him.

Guidelines can even be helpful in heading off noise issues. Talk to your prospective tenant about noise issues. Let him know that you expect him to be reasonably quiet. I am upfront enough to say, *"If you are wanting to have loud parties, or play loud music, this is not the place for you. We are looking for a quiet tenant."* If he has teenage children, I ask about who will be in control of the volume of the music. If I allow a dog, I discuss the issue of a barking dog and what they will do if this becomes a problem for the neighbors.

Find a Spy

This might sound a bit James Bondish, but a good spy is invaluable in keeping alert as to what is going on in your rental. You don't live there, so you only have a murky idea of what really goes on after the agreement is signed. You can only drive by so many times on a Friday or Saturday night to gauge the noise level or count the number of cars in the driveway. When a tenant complains about another tenant, you are only hearing one side of the story. A known neighbor or a long-term tenant in your apartment building can really help you know if trouble is brewing.

A helpful neighbor once called to ask us if we knew that our small out-of-town two-bedroom rental was housing at least a dozen people. No we did not.

"Did you know that the tenants in Apt. A have had their electricity turned off for non-payment and are burning candles at night for light?" phoned in one alert tenant. I was happy to have this information before it resulted in a call from the fire department.

Another time we were told that a tenant had illegally rented out a back room and that the renters were using an outside bedroom window to enter and exit so as not to draw attention to their new living arrangement.

Often it is a neighbor who phones and tells me that the police were called to a rental the night before to quiet down a loud party or a domestic dispute. Somehow the problem tenant never feels compelled to share this information with me.

Value your spy and let them know you appreciate the inside information. It can save you big time down the line. Never, never reveal the identity of your spy to those ratted out, or you might just start a brand new feud of epic proportions. Let the spy remain anonymous at all times. The problem tenant doesn't need to know how you know. Your problem tenant may ask, *"Who told you?"* But you can usually evade the question by saying something like, *"It is my job to know what going on in my rentals."*

Safety First

The best way to keep your tenants secure and to head off a potential lawsuit, it to make sure that your rentals are safe and sanitary. I actually have a pretty good track record in this area. Only one lawsuit so far—and it was fraudulent. I treat my tenants with respect and keep each rental in a condition that I would be happy to live in.

Check periodically to be sure your rentals and rental property are in good repair. Keep utilities up to code. Don't allow the use of a lot of extension cords or an overloading of the electrical circuit. Be sure gas heaters are properly vented. Remove or repair any jagged or broken pieces of a wood or metal fencing. It is always worth it to replace or repair anything that is dangerous or below standard. Railings, stairs, sidewalks, appliances, electrical outlets must all be in top working order. See Chapter 10 on "Improvements and Repairs" for more specifics.

In the rental business, an ounce of prevention is worth a pound of cure. This way no tenant is likely to be injured on your property or have grounds for a lawsuit. Keep your rentals up, treat your tenants fairly, honor your end of the rental agreement, and no tenant will have a legitimate feud with you.

Know When to Say When

Try not to get into the middle of tenant feuds. Often tenants can work out their difficulties among themselves. Their fighting children become best friends, they decide to trade off the lawn mowing responsibilities, the feuding couple goes to counseling or gets divorced.

I do step in when safety is an issue. If a tenant is burning candles in place of electricity, or selling pills to the neighboring druggies, or has tried to run down his neighbor with his car, things need to be resolved right away.

When a tenant becomes a real problem for you or for his neighboring tenants, it is time to start an eviction. It is far better to get rid of the problem tenant than to lose your good tenants. One really obnoxious or dangerous tenant can cause a whole apartment building to vacate. So know when to say *"That's enough!"* See Chapter 13 for details about eviction.

You can avoid many tenant conflicts by good planning on your part. You cannot however ultimately control the behavior of your tenants. You cannot control tenants who choose to fight with their spouse or with their neighbors, or decide to break the law.

What you can control is how much bad behavior you are willing to put up with. You can control if illegal or excessively loud or obnoxious activity will continue to be allowed to occur on your property. You hold the trump card of eviction.

By following these guidelines, you will be doing what you can to set the stage for your tenants to be happy and to avoid fusses and feuds on your property. Good fences may not make good neighbors, but good landlording practices just might.

Avoiding Feuds Checklist

- ❑ Select a good tenant.
- ❑ Pick tenants with similar life styles to live in close proximity with each other.
- ❑ Divide available space fairly among tenants.
- ❑ Set down ground rules for space and noise issues.
- ❑ Find a good spy.
- ❑ Keep rentals safe.
- ❑ Evict a problem tenant before you lose your good tenants.

You are the Landlord…If you can keep your rental addresses out of the police Rolodex you're on a roll.

*This form is found in the back of this book.

Chapter 13

Eviction

Sixty (60) Day Notice to Quit

*TENANT(S)*_____

PREMISES _____

Street Address

_____

City	*State*	*Zip Code*

TO TENANT (S) AND ALL PERSONS IN POSSESSION:

YOU ARE HEREBY NOTIFIED that the tenancy under which you occupy the premises shall end sixty (60) days after the date of service of a copy of this notice upon you, and you are required to quit and deliver up possession of the premises to the undersigned on or before that date.

IF YOU FAIL TO DO SO, legal proceedings will be instituted against you for possession of the premises, for forfeiture of the rental agreement, and for such monetary damages as may be allowed by law.

Dated this _____day of _____, 20_____.

_____

Owner/Agent

This is a **Sixty Day Notice to Quit*

Eviction

How to Get Rid of the Tenant from Hell

From time to time you will discover that you have seriously misjudged a tenant. Your best detective work failed to uncover the fact that he is a deadbeat. You have rented to someone who cannot pay the rent and who will not do the right thing and move out. Actually he has no place to go and no money to go there. He will most likely choose to stay in your rental until forced out by a legal eviction.

How did you get into this fix? Nearly 80 % of all evictions start with the failure to review the rental application. You got in a hurry to rent your unit. The tenant looked good up front and on paper, so you didn't check his reference, or more importantly—his credit report.

Somehow in the rental application he forgot to mention his forced evictions from the last three places where he rented. When you finally ran that credit check after three bounced rent checks, you found that he had no credit history, or that he has bad credit from a checkered past. Either that, or he is renting under an assumed name. His social security number is non-existent too. But he and the several guests he has moved into your rental are all too real. As real as the latest high-end utility bills. He's not paying any rent but legally you can't just throw him and his friends out or even shut off the water.

OK—so you've made a slight misstep. Don't beat yourself up over it. The tenant will take care of that for you. We all make mistakes, and this one will cost you; but it will be worth it to break company with a real loser who's bleeding you dry. This is one of the occasions for which you have that little reserve account saved up in the bank.

To make things right, you will need an eviction attorney. I am not a lawyer. I am a landlord. Therefore, I cannot give you legal advice. I can only shine a little light on the bumpy path ahead. Take my advice and hire an attorney.

Symptoms of Trouble in Paradise

The first symptom of impending trouble in paradise is when the rent doesn't arrive on time, or when it doesn't arrive at all. You phone the tenant and hear the first of many excuses. *The check is in the mail. I needed to do some car repairs. I'm off work on a temporary disability. My alimony check was late.* If this happens once and then straightens out, it might be a fluke. But most often, this is the start of the slide into acute non-payment of rent. Even worse is when you phone the tenant about the missing rent and get his answering machine time after time. The tenant never calls back. You are being seriously ignored.

If the tenant **is** speaking to you—next you will begin hearing from him the many heartbreaking excuses, extenuating circumstances, and life changing events that have make it problematic for him to pay the rent. Sympathy is nice, however, you are the one left holding the bounced checks and still needing to make the mortgage payment. The tenant's problems have quickly become your problem. The promise of payment "next week" begins to blur into "next month."

Often you discover that the tenant in trouble isn't giving you the true story. He might not think paying the rent is a high priority. He often fails to mention his drug or alcohol problem, the loss of his job, the warrant out for his arrest, or the gambling debts that have a stranglehold on his finances.

I've never had a tenant in trouble say to me, *"I'm very sorry, but this is the start of a period of at least six months where I will be unable to pay the rent. Since I can't keep my part of the rental agreement, here is my notice. I'll move out right away and stay with relatives until my situation improves."* Instead, most tenants in financial trouble will string you along from month-to-month always promising that relief is just around the corner. I used to believe them.

Failure to Pay the Rent

The first sign that there might be a problem is the non-payment of the rent. You know you are looking at a serious problem when any or all of the following happen: if a tenant has not paid the rent by the 15th of the month for a rent due on the 1st of the month; if he has not satisfied you that he is having temporary problems and will pay the rent in the near future; if he is not returning your phone calls; if he has a pattern of late payment; if you believe he is unable or unwilling to meet his commitment to pay the rent on time and in full. At this point you should seriously consider starting an eviction. Hoping for the best is prone to disappointment.

Lying

Jack was a good tenant for a number of years. Then his drinking began to get the better of him. He went through a divorce. His work suffered. He stopped paying his rent on time. When I would phone, he had a lot of excuses and promised to run the rent right over. He came over, but only with a partial payment. *"I'll bring the rest on Monday,"* he promised. Monday came and went, and no money was forthcoming. Jack paid in fits and starts, never fully catching up on what he owed. He was soon months behind in his rent. I began a separate ledger to keep track of the balance owed. I wrote him letters detailing exactly how much he was in arrears, requesting payment in full.

After six months of this little game we ended up in court. Jack hired an attorney to fight the eviction. In his testimony he claimed, *"It was just so confusing, she never told me what I owed."* He tried to use the rent receipts for his partial payments to claim that I had accepted that amount as payment in full. In front of the judge, Jack criticized my accounting, my rental, and me. According to his lawyer, I was the bad guy. His client was pure as driven snow. There is something about being called a bungler and a liar in a court of law that is deeply humiliating. Being maligned in court was my reward for tying to be patient with Jack and his problems.

In the end, the judge knew a snow job when he saw one. I got a judgment for the $8000+ owed in back rent and legal fees. Jack finally moved out of our rental and much more quickly moved out of state. I hired an attorney there to track him down, in hopes of collecting on the judgment. I never got a penny. Misplaced hope can be costly.

Intimidation

Sometimes a tenant in financial trouble will try to intimidate you by becoming hostile and aggressive. He tries to make you feel like the bad guy for not trusting him and for being so concerned about getting paid.

Mr. Necktie began having trouble paying his rent, and I began to have trouble tracking him down. Apparently he found my phone inquiries about the unpaid rent to be bothersome and petty.

"Well…I've been out of town on important business. How was I supposed to pay the rent? Why are you so worried? Don't you know I lead a busy professional life?"

According to Mr. Necktie, his check was in the mail, but it never seemed to arrive. The checks that did come began to bounce. When I called to report the latest "insufficient funds" notice. Mr. Necktie snapped back, *"Well…if it will make you feel any better, I'll send you a money order."* The issue was not about feeling better, but about actually getting paid. With a smug air of superiority, Mr. Necktie implied that I was needlessly questioning his character.

I called one afternoon after another missed rent deadline and his housemate (who was just a guest) told me that the tenant was out fishing. That night my husband and I arrived on his doorstep to ask about his unpaid rent. Mr. Necktie was outraged that we wanted to get paid.

He began screaming that he was about to give <u>us</u> notice. *The rental had mold…he had been sick for weeks. Couldn't we see how red his face was? We'd be luck if he didn't sue….* I wondered if he could actually sue us for the sunburn he got from fishing on the lake.

We went home without the rent and I phoned our eviction attorney. Mr. Necktie was served the next day. When we were cleaning up his house after the eviction, I opened a drawer. It was filled with unpaid bills. Most of them were never opened. I guess the check was in the mail.

The Hot Check

Miss Betty thought nothing of writing me a hot check. She was sure it would get me off her case for a few weeks until it came back "insufficient funds" from her credit union. When I finally tracked down her bank, I was able to take the rent check there directly and thus avoid 10 days of suspense. In an attempt to stave off an eviction, Betty's mother began to pay her rent. But soon her savings were depleted.

This game of cat, mouse and mother went on for several months. Miss Betty could be hostile when confronted and wouldn't let me in to check out her apartment, even after a **24 Hour Right of Inspection Notice*** had been given. Perhaps she didn't want me to detect her 5 unauthorized cats and her live-in boyfriend. Betty had no trouble breaking all the rules. Finally I had had enough. I began the eviction and Miss Betty called to personally cuss me out on the phone. She ignored every legal notice and stretched out her tenure as far as possible. Because of her many delaying tactics, Betty's eviction date fell just after Christmas.

In a final attempt at manipulation, I received a tearful call from Miss Betty on (you guessed it) Christmas Eve. Maybe in the season of light and peace, she thought she could buy a little more time. *"What am I going to do?"* she sobbed. I wish she had asked this question 6 months earlier before all those bounced checks and months of unpaid rent. My forced charity to her cause had not been appreciated or acknowledged.

Was Betty entitled to free bed and board? Should fraud, nastiness and rule breaking and cussing out your landlord be rewarded? Was I responsible to support Betty, her boyfriend and her lifestyle forever? I guess in her mind, possession meant entitlement. I was sorry for her dire straits, but Miss Betty had brought them on herself, and in the process had milked me for time and money, and plenty of emotional distress. I didn't need another work-over on Christmas Eve.

Miss Betty began to rant. *"Am I supposed to just throw my couch over the balcony…I have nowhere to go! It's all your fault. You are mean…hateful…(and a few other words I'll not include here.)"*

In the end Betty repaid us for the many extended rent-free months in our rental by trashing the apartment, removing the litter box and letting her 4 unauthorized cats urinate and defecate on the carpets (totally ruining them and the hardwood floors underneath), making us haul and store her abandoned property for the full term, and leaving us with a full dumpster load of junk and garbage to haul away.

Nobody is happy to have to be involved in an eviction. But where promises are thin, the law steps in. This is why landlords have to develop a thick skin.

Breach of the Rental Agreement

Sometimes the tenant manages to pay the rent, but has other problems that cause you to decide an eviction is necessary. Usually these problems involve flagrant violations of your rental agreement. The tenant might have moved in unauthorized guests, pets, or vehicles. He might be damaging your rental. He might be using your rental as a place to sell drugs, have loud parties, or to conduct a business. When warnings to comply with the terms of the agreement fail, an eviction is the best way to gain back control of your rental.

Miss Party-Hearty used to be a responsible mother of three. Then came the fights. Then came the drugs. Then the divorce. Then the live-in boyfriend. Soon our nice little rental was party-central. It filled with partying strangers high on alcohol and drugs every weekend. The police became familiar with the address. When Miss Party-Hearty and her boyfriend got really strung out, they had knockdown drag-out fights, which not only roused all the neighbors from their sleep, but also somehow tore each and every door in the house off its hinges. This was one tenant on whom we were glad to close and lock the newly repaired doors after an eviction. For us the parting if not the partying was sweet.

We've had our share of evictions but they are become much more rare as we do that more thorough tenant and credit checks **before** renting. Now only about one out of every thirty tenancies ends in eviction. We've learned the hard way that an ounce of prevention is worth a pound of cure meted out in court.

Eviction Hall of Infamy

Just in case you're not sufficiently convinced of the perils of eviction, I asked my eviction attorney for his worst eviction horror stories. Here they are.

A father who I'll call Poppy rented a nice three-bedroom house to his daughter and son-in-law and their three children. Poppy charged them only $350 per month. But soon his relatives got involved in drug deals on the property. Drug Enforcement contacted Poppy and insisted he evict his children or the agency would seize his property. The kids fought the eviction. They claimed he had given the property over to them.

After the trial, the property was awarded to Poppy, but the angered kids weren't done yet. They filled socks with concrete and flushed them down the toilets. They bashed holes in all the walls and cut up the wiring with bolt cutters. They next went to the store and bought 50 pounds of fish, which they stashed in the attic. It was a very hot July. Then they smashed up all the countertops and fixtures. As a final parting shot, they taped up the doors, turned on all the faucets and left by a tall window. When Poppy and the sheriff arrived, they pried open the front door and were deluged with a two foot wall of water, a very bad smell, and the fateful knowledge that blood isn't necessarily thicker than water.

Another disgruntled tenant blew up the house on his way out. He set a delayed fuse and turned on the gas and closed the door behind him.

Eviction, as you can see, can be a real powder keg.

Getting it Right

Grounds for Eviction

While non-payment of rent is the most common cause for an eviction proceeding, other reasons to consider an eviction are if the tenant is in serious violation of other portions of the **Rental Agreement***. Is the rental being damaged by too many people living there? Has your tenant brought in pets in spite of signing a "no pets" agreement? Has the tenant started having loud fights or parties? You can lose your good tenants in an apartment building for instance, by not removing out-of-control tenants who are loud and unruly, especially at night.

What legally constitutes grounds for an eviction? Any serious breach of the rental agreement can be considered grounds for eviction. The problem is that you have to prove these grounds in a court of law. Can you prove that your tenant actually has a dog? Can you provide evidence that he smokes in the house? Can you prove that three people not listed in your rental agreement actually live there? Can you show that the tenant has loud parties on a regular basis? Can you verify that he is bothering the neighbors with his loud music? Can you prove that he is dealing drugs out of your rental?

Because these areas are so hard to substantiate—even if you know them to be true, it is best to just begin an eviction without stating a specific reason. By law, you are not required to give a reason for an eviction, as long as the tenant's month-to-month term or one-year lease period is over. This is where you realize the beauty of the month-to-month rental agreement. With this tenancy you can just give a 30-day or a 60-day notice. On the other hand, if you have gone with the yearlong lease and want to get rid of a tenant earlier, you will have to prove cause or wait until the lease period is up.

If you do state a reason for the eviction, the easiest thing to prove is non-payment of the rent. In this case the tenant will have no cancelled checks or written rent receipts from you as evidence that the rent has been paid. You should have documents showing that you asked for payment of the rent but did not receive it. This means that you should send a letter to the tenant asking for the unpaid rent with the amount specified. Keep a copy of this letter for your records. Other legal notices like the **3-Day Pay or Quit Notice*** will also state the amount of unpaid rent.

Decide if an Eviction is What You Want

An eviction proceeding is a legal way to remove a tenant from your rental. Is this what you want? Remember that this is a costly and time-consuming process, which will probably require you to appear in court with your records.

Sometimes you may decide that you want to give a good tenant a bit more time to pay the rent, or to get rid of that unauthorized pet. Sometimes you really do believe his hard luck story and that things will be better in a few weeks or months.

Candy, a new tenant, was pregnant when she and her husband moved into our three-bedroom house. Six months later, pregnancy complications forced Candy to take a leave from work for a time of bed rest before her son was born. Suddenly, Candy and her husband were unable to pay the rent. Her parents helped with the next month's rent. Then Candy sent a post-dated check, which we held for 15 days only to have it bounce. It was rough going for about three months, during which time they fell behind in the rent. After the baby was born, Candy returned to work, and the rent payments got back on track. As Candy is a good tenant, it was worth bearing with some unexpected bumps in the road.

On the other hand, if you have a questionable tenant who is chronically late with the rent, one who is not paying the rent, or a tenant who is damaging your rental—consider starting an eviction before things go from bad to worse. Do you really think that the partying will stop, or that the many pets will go, or that this time the job will last? Or are this tenant's many problems creating a no-win situation for you?

The alternative is to wait and hope. But each month that goes by without a payment of rent is income most likely forever lost to you. If you decide to extend grace, remember that there is a good possibility that the tenant may never shape up or pay you the rent owed. Delaying the start of an eviction process gives him more free time in your rental. And if he is in a bad mood, your allowing him more time to seriously damage your rental.

The average uncontested eviction process takes from three to five weeks. If it is contested it can take from six to a full eight weeks. It can take even longer if the tenant uses stalling tactics like declaring bankruptcy. Usually you are receiving no rent during this time. During an eviction process you are, in effect, supporting your tenant by providing his housing and some utilities. This is not what you agreed to do. Nor can you afford to do this on a regular basis and stay in the rental business. Remember that this is a business, not a welfare agency.

So, in general I suggest you cut your losses and start an eviction proceeding at the first serious sign of trouble—the non-payment of rent.

Stay in Charge

Once you have decided that an eviction is necessary, stay in charge of the process. Your tenant might say that he's going to move out. Don't believe him. You still need to get the legal process started to ensure that he does.

Sometimes a tenant will try to call the shots by saying something like, *"I hate it here! I'm giving you notice. I'll be out as soon as I find a new place."* For his notice to be legal, it must be in writing and must state a specific date of departure.

Accepting a vague verbal notice leaves you at his mercy. If you don't know when or if the tenant if leaving, you have no way to plan for the future of your rental. After a vacancy, you will need to clean, advertise, re-rent the unit. It should be on your timetable—not his. If a tenant gives this kind of vague *I'm moving* talk and especially if he starts running out his security deposit as a last month's rent, give him notice. This way the time clock is ticking legally. You have some control over when he leaves, and you are not left hanging until if or when he happens to find a better place.

Another scenario is when the tenant has given you a 30-day written notice. But after the 30 days he is still there. In this case you can use his own notice to allow you to go to the **Unlawful Detainer**. (See Step 2 under the Eviction Process section of this chapter) Maybe the tenant still wants to move but needs a few more days or another month for a house construction or another rental to be ready. In this case, if you are willing to have him stay, you can remain in charge by rewriting the 30-day notice for the extended period, having him sign a new rental agreement and most importantly pay the extra month's rent up front. Don't allow him to use the security deposit as you may need it for repairs or extended unpaid rent. Keep everything in writing and you have a legal document.

Hire an Eviction Attorney

The best way to stay in charge of an eviction is to get good advice from a professional attorney who specializes in evictions. When you believe that an eviction is necessary, start with a good eviction attorney. You should <u>not</u> try to handle an eviction on your own. To do this you would have to know how to present and enter evidence in a court of law, answer objections, counter with the law and conduct your own case. An eviction is a legal matter and one misstep on your part can cause delay and loss of money. An eviction is a little like a chess match with moves by you and countermoves by your tenant. You want to win back possession of your property. If you miss a step in the process, or make a wrong move, you will have to start over from square one.

Chances are, your problem tenant has already sought legal advice about how to make the most of his free rent. In fact, in many counties, when your case is filed your tenant will receive notice in the mail of the lawsuit and be given a list of where to obtain free legal aid. You need an attorney to advise you of your rights and those of your tenant. You need an attorney to walk you through the steps of the legal process. An attorney can not only advise you of each step needed, he can serve the papers, thus sparing you emotional aggravation and possible physical harm. You need an attorney to keep you from making a costly mistake. You may need him to hold your hand. He knows how frustrating this process can be. He believes you when you say your tenant is a deadbeat. He knows how you can prove it. He is on your side in court.

I am not an eviction attorney. I am a landlord. I cannot give you legal advice. What follows is a rough outline of the eviction process to give you a sense of the process involved. It is not meant to be legal advice. Hire an attorney. You will need one.

To find a good attorney, choose one who specializes in rental evictions. This is a specialized field with changing rules and regulations for each state. You can get a referral from a property management company. Find an attorney who is willing to take the time to talk to you, walk you through the process, and prepare a strategy with you for any courtroom appearances. Most attorneys charge a set fee for each document needed, for process serving, and for court appearances.

Starting the Process

First, you need to decide if you want to get rid of this tenant no matter what, or if you would settle for just getting the rent. If you think the tenant might shape up, you can start with a **3-Day Pay or Quit Notice***. This is the first step of an eviction, and lets your tenant know that you are serious about being paid.

Notices of this sort should be taken to the property. You should knock on the door and attempt to personally deliver the notice to the tenant, or hire a server through your attorney to do it for you. If there is no answer you may post the notice on the front door. If the notice is not hand delivered to the tenant, you will also need to mail a copy of the notice by first class mail.

In theory, this means that the tenant has three days to pay the rent or he should quit living in your rental. In reality it means that if he does not pay the rent within a 3-day period after receipt of your notice, you will begin the rest of the eviction process.

However, if the tenant does pay up the rent, you will have to start all over again if you want to evict him at a later time. He is back to square one—back to being a tenant in good standing. Also be aware that if you accept any money from the tenant at this stage, even an amount less than the full rent, you have to start with another notice.

Sometimes, you don't want to settle for just getting the rent paid after a legal threat. You have seen the handwriting on the wall and you just want to get rid of a bad tenant—no matter what. Maybe he is dealing drugs out of your rental. Maybe you have to beg for the rent each month and he is getting seriously behind. Maybe he keeps the neighbors on edge with late night fights and numerous guests. Maybe the dog he claims not to have barks all day while he is at work. Maybe your rental is sustaining some serious damage ranging from broken windows to a dangerous accumulation of trash. Maybe your sweet little studio has a dozen people in residence. Maybe your tenant has run out of excuses and you have run out of patience. In spite of your best efforts to resolve the problems, you have reached the end. You want him out whether he pays the rent or not. It is time to start an eviction.

The Eviction Process

An eviction is the legal process by which you gain back possession of your rental property and obtain a judgment for any rent owed, damages, and legal expenses.

Your eviction attorney will first want to look at a copy of the signed **Rental Agreement*** you have for this tenant. The legal system can only enforce what is legally in writing. This is why it is important to have a good rental agreement, which has been dated and signed by you and your tenant.

This is also why you need to have a good filing system and good record keeping about the payment of rent. Always keep the **Rental Agreement***, and **Addendum*** and any changes to it (such as a rent increase) filed in a safe place. Keep accurate records of any rents paid by check. Always give out a written receipt for rent payments made in cash and keep a copy of this receipt for your records. Good records beat relying on *he said/she said* any day.

Now, The Game Begins:
Step One

First you must give the tenant notice that an eviction process is starting. If you are willing to keep the tenant if he pays up the rent, you can start with the **3-Day Pay or Quit Notice***. This dated notice lists the tenant's name and address, the amount of rent owed, and the period for which it is owed. It can be hand delivered or if attached to the tenant's door must also be mailed to the tenant. This gives him three days (3 days from the delivery of the notice) to pay up his rent.

The other type of notice is a **30-Day Notice*** or a **60-Day Notice***. If a tenant has rented from you for less than a year and is on a month-to-month rental agreement, you can give him a **30-Day Notice*** for any reason. If he has rented from you for a year or longer, then you must start with a **60-Day Notice***. You can also give notice at the expiration of a fixed term lease. If you are not willing to keep this tenant even if he pays up the rent, or if the tenant is current in the rent, and you want to evict him for another reason, this is your first step. If the tenant fails to move within this 30 or 60-day period you move on to the next step.

Hire a Process Server

I think that it pays to hire a server through your eviction attorney to serve these notices. This saves you having to have a face-to-face confrontation with an often-angry tenant. The server is an unbiased (and unrecognized) party who can hand the legal document to your tenant. This prevents the danger to you from a disgruntled or violent tenant. A legal server is trained in how to protect himself. For purposes of serving the notices, your eviction attorney will ask you for some details like what the tenant looks like, if you would expect him to be hostile, what kind of car he drives and what hours he is likely to be found at home.

Step Two

Now, an **Unlawful Detainer** is filed. This means that the tenant is unlawfully in your rental. He has not paid his rent, or has not moved out as required by law after his 30 or 60-day notice. Your tenant has 5 days to respond to the **Unlawful Detainer Notice** if it is personally served. If it is sub-served (given to another party at the address) your tenant has 15 days in which to respond. You will also want to cover any other John Does who might be living there. A John Doe is a person who is living in your rental without your knowledge or permission. Your tenant may have moved in a boyfriend, girlfriend, adult child, or guest without informing you. You many not know his identify or even his name. You may be blissfully unaware of his existence. This mystery guest, however, has rights, so you must cover yourself legally for this possibility. Any John Doe living in your rental has 10 days to respond.

You tenant must respond to the court. He fills out a form and gives his answer to the lawsuit you have filed against him. Fees are required for your filing and for his response. Only about 30% of tenants in an eviction will answer to the court following the **Unlawful Detainer**. Most do it to buy time. It gives them an additional 2 weeks in your rental.

Step Three

The court will then set a trial date for this case. This is usually set for within 20 days of the tenant response to the lawsuit. This is considered a fast-track case as monetary damages (to you) are accruing at a daily rate.

Step Four

Next you go to trial. Your lawyer presents your case and defends you against any arguments your tenant and his attorney may have. You may have to take the stand, be sworn in, and testify. Your records may be used as evidence. The judge will make his decision. If all goes well, you will be awarded possession. At this time you might also be given a judgment for money owed to you by the tenant.

Only about half of tenants involved in an eviction proceeding will actually show up in court. If he fails to show, you will still need to do a default prove-up. This means that in the absence of the tenant your attorney will have to present evidence for an eviction showing things like the non-payment of rent, the proper notices given etc. Your attorney will then ask for a judgment.

The Judgment

If the judge at the eviction hearing rules in your favor, you can be given a judgment for back rent owned and possibly for damages to your rental property. A **judgment**, however, is not a **payment** of money owed to you. Trying to collect on the judgment is a whole 'nother process. You can try to have an attorney attach wages from your former tenant or get money from an existing bank account. But these methods are far from a sure thing. I have never collected on a judgment. The tenant either has no job, no money, or he skips town leaving you with a worthless judgment.

Step Five

If the tenant still does not move out, after the judgment and legal awarding of your property back to you, you can call for a sheriff to come and physically remove the tenant from your property. It usually takes eight working days after the decision for the sheriff to come.

Now you are back in possession of your property. You must however follow the law in properly storing or disposing of any abandoned property left behind by this tenant. See Chapter 15 for detailed instructions on how to deal with any abandoned property.

Calling in the Sheriff

The final step of an eviction (if it goes this far) is the actual arrival of the sheriff who will physically remove the tenant from the building. You will receive notice of when the sheriff is scheduled to arrive and will be instructed to have a locksmith come at the same time to change the locks. This effectively bars the tenant from re-entering your property.

You wouldn't think that a tenant would actually wait for this step to leave, but some people are big on denial and wishful thinking.

Miss Bliss fought the eviction all the way. She didn't have any money for rent, but she somehow secured the best legal advice on how to prolong her say in our little Shangri-La. Every move on the eviction chessboard was met with a brilliant counter move. We move a rook, she jockeyed a bishop. Her last ditch and intentionally last minute move of bankruptcy was processed just as the sheriff, a locksmith and we humble landlords had gathered at the front door. A phone call on the sheriff's cell phone announced that we were stymied again. Her filing had bought her a full month's reprieve.

But at last it was checkmate. Having exhausted all legal excuses to delay the inevitable, it was time to go. The sheriff arrived (again) at 10:00 am. Miss Bliss was unbelievably still in bed. *"You really think this is fun, don't you?"* Miss Bliss snarled as she was rousted out of her bed. There was a certain amount of satisfaction in reaching the end of the game, but I wouldn't call it fun.

Listen to Your Attorney

Besides advising you during the process, your attorney can also be helpful by securing a process server to serve the needed notices to your tenant, and he will represent you in court.

Remember my advice. Hire an attorney. It will be wise to spend some money now to avoid getting ripped off by your tenant later. Don't try to take shortcuts or take matters into your own hands.

Your attorney is trained to know the steps needed and how to head off possible legal problems. My attorney has advised me about such important details as listing the tenant's names and *"any and all occupants"* on the forms just in case a mystery guest is living there. Believe it or not, a mystery guest has rights—rights to stay in your rental if not properly legally addressed.

My attorney has also saved my case and my sanity by telling me when I should and should not accept money from a tenant. He keeps me on track and appraised of the step-by-step progress of the case. He lets me whine once in a while. He assures me that in the end the tenant will have to get out. He gives me a timeline, a court date, and the assurance that with patience and the right legal moves the eviction will be successful.

A Reasonable Bribe?

If things are going from bad to worse in your rental and you'd like to speed up the eviction process, you can try a bribe. After the first eviction notice has been delivered, the tenant knows you are serious about getting him out. He also knows and can be reminded that according to **Section 16** of your **Rental Agreement*** he will be liable for any legal and court costs incurred in getting him out.

Section 16. If any legal action or proceeding be brought by either party to enforce any part of this agreement, the prevailing party shall recover any reasonable attorney's fees and costs, in addition to all other relief.

Therefore your tenant might be willing to get out sooner with a small bribe. You could for example offer him $300-$500 in cash if he has totally vacated the house, leaving it in good condition, by a certain date, one that is say, within the week. Or you could offer to pay his moving costs if he meets your deadline and cleans up the house. If he moves out quickly, before going to court, you will come out ahead financially.

I know…I know…. Giving a bribe to get rid of a bad tenant may feel a bit galling to you, but think of an eviction as a divorce. Two parties are splitting up. Hard feeling are involved. Your tenant has less to lose than you do. If he agrees, it will save both of you time, money and aggravation. It will cost a lot more to go to court. In the meantime, keep on with the eviction process, just in case he doesn't follow through. Only give him the money after he has totally moved out and you have changed the locks. You will, of course, forfeit any possible legal judgment by cutting short the legal process, but you will usually gain possession faster and save money on legal fees. It will be a stalemate, but the game is over.

Keeping Your Cool

It helps to take a few deep breaths and long walks during this process. An eviction is by nature an emotional event. You've been burned. You feel like crying and yelling and giving the jerk a piece of your mind for taking away your peace of mind—not to mention a large piece of your cash. I found myself getting angry just writing this chapter. My blood pressure went up as I relived some of the more excruciating moments of tenant flameout. Deep breath...relax. Try not to take it personally.

So try and keep your cool during the process. Don't call up the tenant from hell and read him the riot act. Don't write him angry letters that can be used against you in court. Don't drive by and give him a rude gesture or receive one from him. Don't have any contact at all. Be cool. Be civilized. Be the bigger person. Behave.

The less contact you have with your tenant during this time the better. An angry tenant can tear up your rental, punch holes in the walls and do mean things like flushing large objects down the toilet to get back at you as he leaves.

Forget about revenge. The problem tenant has to live with himself. You can start fresh with a new renter and hopefully a better experience.

The End Result

The final result you are looking for in an eviction is to get the bad tenant out of your rental house in the shortest amount of time with the least amount of monetary, physical and emotional damage to you and to your rental. Be happy just to get the tenant out even if you never collect on the judgment for back rent.

Let your attorney and the legal system work. Keep your eyes on the prize. It may seem painstakingly slow, but in the end you will win. You progress move by careful move on the eviction chessboard until...Checkmate at last. You win! You are back in control of your rental property. An eviction is not fun, but it is your recourse for the deadbeat tenant.

Eviction Checklist

- ❑ Decide if an eviction is what you want.
- ❑ Determine what grounds you have for eviction or if you will not state a reason.
- ❑ Hire an eviction attorney.
- ❑ Start the legal process.
- ❑ Stay in charge of the process.
- ❑ Complete each step of the eviction:
    1. **3 day Pay or Quit*** and/or a **30 day** or **60 day Notice to Quit***
    2. **Unlawful Detainer**
    3. Trial Date
    4. Possession and Judgment
    5. Calling in the Sheriff
- ❑ Keep your cool.
- ❑ You Win!

You are the Landlord...be happy it's just a tenant, not a relative.

*This form is found at the back of this book.

Chapter 14

The Security Deposit

The Tenant shall deposit with the Owner, as a security deposit, the sum of $_____, payable
_____.

*The Security Deposit amount is **not** a last month's rent and may not be used as such.*

The Owner may claim and withhold from the Security Deposit only such amounts as are reasonably necessary to remedy Tenant defaults as follows:

a. for payment of rent, or

b. to repair damages to the premises caused by the Resident, exclusive of ordinary wear and tear, or

c. to clean such premises, if necessary, upon termination of the tenancy.

No later than two weeks (14 days) after the Tenant has vacated the premises, the Owner shall furnish the Tenant with an itemized written statement of the basis for, and the amount of, any security received and disposition of such security and shall return any remaining portion of such security to the Tenant.

For this purpose, the Tenant is requested to leave with the Owner a forwarding address upon vacating the rental.*

This form is from the **Rental Agreement.*

Where it's Supposed to Go...
Where it Really Goes

In an ideal world, the security deposit is supposed to provide the Landlord with a little security against things like unpaid rent and holes in the walls. In the actual world, the tenant sees this deposit as **his** security blanket, which will allow him to run it out as a last month's rent while saving his money toward renting the next place. You see the dilemma. Each party has his own agenda for this little nest egg.

When leaving the nest of your rental, the tenant might make a real effort to clean up, or he might just fly the coop and leave the poop (sometimes literally) behind. Once the tenant has vacated the premises, you may find that he has vacated his promises as well.

A few short years ago, he promised to love, cherish, and actually clean your rental. *"I leave a place better than I found it,"* he said with a note of pride in his voice. Now as you survey the wreckage, you notice that the carpet is beyond repair, and the only "better" or is it worse thing he has left behind is the pile of old clothes, furniture and mattresses. He has, of course, run out most of his security deposit as his last month's rent, and you have very little left to pay for cleaning, repair, and hauling away his unwanted discards. You are not feeling very secure at all as you mentally tabulate how much it will cost to get your rental in top shape once again.

I Feel Sooo Secure

The security deposit is supposed to encourage the tenant to clean up when he moves out. It is a little incentive to not only move everything out, but to vacuum as well. But, it doesn't always do the job.

Cynthia, the hapless mother of a supposedly adult tenant showed up to move out some of his left behind items. Her son apparently had not told her about his eviction or about all the money he still owed us. His security deposit was long gone and he still owed us several thousand in back rent. Cynthia brightly asked us how much money he would get back if she washed and waxed the floors, after of course making sure the rest of his stuff was hauled away. In a moment of temptation, I toyed with the idea of making up a plausible figure. Cynthia looked like she knew how to mop, and she had a truck. But alas, honesty won out. I never saw Cynthia or her dust mop again…which was a shame. Cynthia's son had left us a real bonanza of rotting garbage and a whole truckload of stuff which we ended up packing and hauling to the dump. I wish he had left us with the security deposit or at the least an enlightened mother with a conscience.

Lucky liked to look on the bright side of every situation. He also like to have a few drinks on a workday evening. He then liked to drive home. It was quite late on one of those nights when I got a call from Lucky. He was calling me from jail. He really needed some bail money. Since I had his security deposit tucked neatly away in my bank account, would I mind running to the County jail with it and springing him loose? I have to give Lucky points for the tenant with the most nerve and the most creative idea for disposing of the security deposit. I think he was a little confused as to just whose security and peace of mind the deposit was supposed to cover.

One tenant liked to smoke in bed. Charlie refused to give up this dangerous practice and assured me that he only smoked outside. One night his smoking ignited the sheets and Charlie was lucky to escape the burning apartment with his life. Surveying the smoldering ruins in his singed pajamas, he lit up a cigarette and asked, *"Does this mean I won't be getting my deposit back?"*

Getting it Right

Calculating the Security Deposit

How much should you ask for a security deposit? In an ideal world you could ask for an amount large enough to actually provide you with security against several months of unpaid rent as well as possible damages of several thousand dollars. But in reality you can't charge such a large amount. So realistically, you need to ask for an amount that equals one month's rent plus an amount for other damages. For example if the rent is $1000 per

month, you would want to collect a security deposit of $1000 plus at least $200 to $500 for damages.

Collecting the Security Deposit

Collecting the security deposit is the first step in creating a hedge against lost rent or damages. If you do not get this deposit up front before the tenant takes possession, you are unlikely to ever get it. So, collect the full amount of the security deposit as well as the first month's rent before you hand over the key. Also, ask for this amount either in cash, a money order, or in a cashier's check. Finding out that the new tenant's check has bounced 10 days after he has taken possession is a poor way to begin your financial relationship.

This step sounds simple enough, but there are pitfalls. This is a lot of money for some people to come up with all at once. They might need $2500 or more to move in to a nice rental. While you can be sympathetic to the prospective tenant's plight, you need to remember that it is now or never. If he cannot raise the money now while the stakes of securing a rental are high, he most likely never will.

One tricky aspect is that the tenant may be waiting to get his security deposit back from the place he is vacating to take your rental. His last landlord, of course, wants him to be totally moved out and wants time to assess damages and make repairs before this money is forthcoming. This is a real dilemma for your tenant, and he will often ask if you will wait until he gets his last deposit back. No you will not. First of all, you do not know how much of a deposit he has coming. There may be some real money coming back or there may not. In the meantime, this person wants to move into your rental. This is where you need to encourage you tenant to get creative. Perhaps a relative who knows this person well will give him a loan until the security deposit is returned. Perhaps he can get a credit card advance. You are not the bank. You are not in the business of giving unsecured loans. You need the money upfront before you can make the deal.

Sometimes a tenant will ask if he can make payments on the security deposit. He might want to pay it over a period of 3-4 months. Your answer is no…No…NO. Remember, you are not the bank. You don't need to take this risk in order to secure a tenant. Once the tenant has possession, he has rights. If you let a tenant in with a small amount or even with a first month's rent plus a portion of the security deposit, you are taking a big chance. If anything goes wrong, you have given over the use or the misuse of your property to someone who won't be that easy to get out.

If your resolve weakens, think about this…. If your proposed tenant can't afford the first month's rent plus the security deposit, what will happen when life happens? What will happen when his car breaks down or his wife takes time off work to have a baby? What will happen when an uncle needs a loan or a child needs braces? What will happen when the dog gets sick, or his employer cuts back on his overtime? I can tell you what will happen. If your tenant is on the edge financially, he will look at paying the rent as an option. Other more pressing obligations will come first. You gave him a no interest, no collateral loan once, surely you can do it again. After all, times are tough.

If a prospective tenant is living so close to the edge that he cannot come up with the security deposit, perhaps he cannot really afford to live in your rental.

Record Keeping

Keep good records on the amount of the security deposit received from each tenant. Most landlords do not keep this money locked up in a separate account, so it is easy to lose track after several years. I record the security amount received on the rental agreement itself, which is carefully filed. When a tenant moves out, it is easy to retrieve this information.

If damages have occurred to the rental, which you have repaired during the tenancy, you will also need to keep the records of receipts and bills involved. For instance if you fixed a broken window or replaced a damaged screen door, put the records in your file to be tallied later against the security deposit.

Damages vs. Wear and Tear

After a tenant moves out, you will need to evaluate the rental and assess damages. This is a good time to get out your **Walk-Through Inspection Sheet** which you have carefully filed with the **Rental Agreement*** and check damaged items against your earlier inventory.

What is considered ordinary wear and tear? What can be considered as damage to the property? This is, of course, somewhat of a judgment call. I always try to bend over backwards to be fair to my tenants.

Consider it normal to need to repaint between tenants, unless they have been in for only a short time. After a tenant moves out, the carpets will need to be cleaned. These two items are a given. This is ordinary wear and tear. But how about cracked tiles on the floor, broken knobs on the stove, or paint splotches on the carpet? If an item will need to be replaced—that is damage. Common items that are broken and need to be replaced are: light fixtures, sink or floor tiles, fan blades, windows, mirrors, mini blinds, vertical blinds, stove knobs, sprinkler heads, and towel racks. More expensive items to replace are cracked sinks, toilets or tubs. This is where it is important to have your inventory handy. A tenant often will say, *"It was broken when I moved in."* You need to be able to say for certain if it was or not.

When you are replacing something used with brand new in a rental, you will need to consider the age of the item and the reason for replacement. Let's say that the carpet was several years old, but was clean and in good shape when the tenant moved in. Now three years later, it has spilled paint on it and pet stains that will not clean out. It would be wrong to assess the full cost of replacing the carpet as it was used when the tenant came in. However, you reasonably expected to get a few more years wear out of the carpet, so you could in good conscience assess a portion of the replacement cost as damages. The damage to the carpeting required you to replace it ahead of schedule.

If a tenant has a cracked a sink, it will need to be replaced. I don't hesitate to charge the full replacement costs as the original sink might have been there indefinitely if not seriously damaged. The same goes for a broken window or nearly-new mini blinds which have been shredded.

Act in Good Faith

I have told the tenant upon move in that I will try to give back the full amount of the deposit if he takes good care of the rental and makes a good effort to clean it after moving out. I really mean it. Most often I do give back the full deposit.

Whenever possible I try to give grace. If a stove knob is missing and I can easily find a replacement, I don't add it to the tab. If the missing fan blade is in the garage and I can reaffix it, no problem. If however, I find the nice vertical blinds ripped off and laying muddied in the side yard, or holes punched in the bedroom doors, I charge full replacement cost.

The leverage of the security deposit is that a tenant who wants to get his deposit back will put in the effort to clean the rental when he leaves. He might actually clean the stove, wash the windows, and even have the carpets cleaned. Prior to move-out I give the tenant a **Tenant Move Out Checklist*** which list the thing I expect to have done if he wants his full security deposit refunded. (See Chapter 15) This way there is no question of what "clean" means. The conscientious tenant knows exactly what he must do to qualify. Sometimes a good tenant leaves a rental in re-rent condition. This is a real plus.

Some landlords give us all a bad name by considering the security deposit as found money. They look for reasons not to give back the deposit. A few spots on the carpet, a few plumbing calls, the need to repaint after a tenancy of five years can all be used as excuses to keep the deposit. Don't be this kind of sleazy landlord. Be prepared to return the full deposit if the tenant has kept up your rental and met the standards of the **Tenant Move Out Checklist*** when vacating your rental.

Running Out the Security Deposit

My **Rental Agreement*** and **Addendum*** clearly state that the security deposit is <u>not</u> a last month's rent and is not to be used for this purpose. In most states it is illegal to charge a last month's rent. I make this concept clear before I accept the deposit. Nevertheless, this is the most common misuse of the security deposit. A tenant who is leaving and who is trying to come up with a security deposit for his next place will often just not pay you the rent for his last month. There goes the bulk of your security deposit. This might work out OK if he moves out on time, and does no damage, but what if he stays for an extra month or two? Now you are really in trouble. Your security deposit is long gone and has just bought time for your tenant. This is especially distressing in the case of an eviction which takes time.

Most often, a tenant is actually moving, but justifies the non payment of the last month's rent because you are, after all, holding **his** money. What he had not taken into account is that repairs can be expensive. Let's say that your security deposit minus the last month's unpaid rent is $300. How far will that really go to replace the carpeting, a broken window and all the mini-blinds in the house? I'm sure you see the problem.

For the tenant this is a win-win situation. He saves money on the last month's rent and doesn't plan on paying for any extensive damages anyway. He'll be long gone without leaving any forwarding address. Unless you track this tenant down and take said tenant to court for damages, you're left holding the repair bills.

I wish I had a solution to this one. I don't. I have to admit that this is one area where the willful tenant always wins. If he chooses not to pay that last month's rent, you're at his mercy. You can just hope and pray that the rental is undamaged. There have been times when the rental was left in good condition and I did give the tenant back the remaining portion of his deposit.

Refunding the Security Deposit

It is a happy day when I can hand back the entire security deposit to a tenant. This has often been the case. I consider this the reward of a good tenant/landlord relationship. I have provided a nice home for the tenant, and the tenant has appreciated it and taken good care of it over time. It has been a mutually rewarding experience.

You can happily hand over the entire security deposit when two conditions have been met. First, the tenant is fully paid up in rent and has not run out any of the security deposit in rent. Secondly, the tenant has not damaged the rental and has followed your guidelines in cleaning it after vacating. I don't get too fussy if the windows haven't been washed, or the toilet needs some calcium removed. In general I like to part ways on a good note.

So if at all possible I give back the total security deposit. Then both tenant and landlord can both be happy campers.

If the security deposit has been run out as a last's months rent or beyond, this amount needs to be deducted from the security deposit.

If damage has occurred to the rental you need to be prompt in having it repaired. Legally you have 14 days after the move out to return the unused portion of the security deposit to the tenant. This is reasonable as otherwise some landlords might stall this off forever. You want to keep the faith with your former tenant and return what you owe him in a prompt manner.

This 14 day period is a little short when you consider that you may need to have work done quickly. Getting a painter in and carpet replaced within two weeks might be a challenge. On the good side, however, the faster the repairs get done, the sooner you can re-rent your unit.

When the repairs and cleanup are done, compile your bills. Add them up and subtract the total from the security deposit. This is the amount you will need to refund to your tenant. You must also supply a written account to the tenant explaining exactly how you used the deposit money. The **Disposition of Security Deposits*** form makes this easy. Fill out the form and mail it to the tenant along with any security deposit refund. Keep a copy for your records. You will also need to enclose copies of the paid bills to verify you expenses. Keep the original bills for your records.

I include the refund check, a filled out **Disposition of Security Deposits*** form and a copy of the paid bills all in the same envelope to the tenant within the 14 day period. If I am giving a full refund of the security deposit, I include the check, and a little note thanking him for being such a good tenant.

If your bills total more than the security amount, you can ask for the money owing, but good luck getting the former tenant to pay the difference. You will still need to sent that disposition letter stating exactly how you used the deposit and stating why he will not be getting a refund. Always keep a copy of this letter of explanation for your files along with the original copy of each bill. In the case of an eviction, this information will be needed in court. If the security deposit money was used as rent, write this out on the form as well.

If you want to be less formal than the **Disposition of Security Deposits*** form, you can compose your own letter explaining what was withheld. A sample letter might look something like this:

Date:_____

Name_____

Address_____

_____

Dear_____

This letter is to explain the disposition of your security deposit. A security deposit in the amount of $2,500_____ was received on Date:_____ for the property known as _____.

This property was vacated on _____20____.

This security deposit was used for the following expenses:

$1000.00 = run out by tenant for May 2003 rent
  325.46 = cost of replacing bathroom sink
  125.63 = cost of replacing light fixtures
   97.46 = cost for cleaning
$1548.55 = TOTAL expenses

$2500.00 security deposit
-1548.55 expenses
  951.55 = Refund amount

Enclosed please find a check in the amount of $_____ which is the balance owed. Copies of the receipts for any repair or cleaning work done on this rental are also enclosed.
   Thank You,
      Signed_____

I bend over backwards to be fair, so I rarely have a tenant question the disposition.

The security deposit does give you some security as your rental changes hands. But don't count on it to meet all your expenses, or to actually secure you from the deadbeat tenant.

In good circumstances you can give back a full refund of this deposit, so make sure you have enough money in the bank to cover this. Learn to be happy when you can give back a full refund of the security deposit. This means that you'll have little cleanup and good thoughts about your last tenant—who was a gem by the way.

Security Deposit Checklist

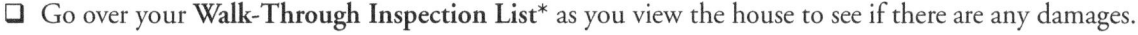

Before Move-In

- ❑ Calculate the Security Deposit needed for each rental.
- ❑ Explain that the Deposit is <u>not</u> a last month's rent.
- ❑ Get the full Security Deposit before giving possession.
- ❑ Keep good records of the deposit.

After Move-Out

- ❑ Go over your **Walk-Through Inspection List*** as you view the house to see if there are any damages.
- ❑ Repair any damages.
- ❑ Clean the rental.
- ❑ Add up the cleaning and repair expenses.
- ❑ Tabulate the balance owed as a refund of the deposit.
- ❑ Send the refund check with the filled out **Disposition of Security Deposit*** form.
- ❑ Send a Thank You note to the good tenant who is getting a full refund.

You are the Landlord…find your security elsewhere.

* This form is found at the back of this book.

Chapter 15

Cleanup & Starting Over

Tenant Move-Out Checklist

Tenant Name_____

Rental Address _____ *CA*_____

Security Deposit Amount $_____ *Received* _____.

As you are ending your tenancy with us we would like to inform you of what is expected by way of move out and cleaning in order to receive back your full Security Deposit refund. We expect to receive back possession of this rental in the same condition in which it was turned over for your use.

This means that the following jobs should be done:

- ❑ *All tenant belongings must be removed from the house, garage and yard. This includes properly disposing of all trash, and removing **anything** brought onto the premises by the tenant. This includes removing items such as wind chimes, bar-b-ques, furniture, appliances, old mattresses, tires, wood, Christmas lights, and empty pots.*
- ❑ *All closets and cupboards are to be totally emptied including the hangers.*
- ❑ *The carpeting must be professionally cleaned. (Do not attempt to clean it yourself with a rented machine, as this may damage the carpet.)*
- ❑ *Any vinyl or wood flooring must be clean and mopped. (Including where the refrigerator has been.)*
- ❑ *The stove and oven must be cleaned.*
- ❑ *Sinks and bathtubs must be scrubbed and free of mildew and soap scum.*
- ❑ *The toilets must be cleaned with no calcium buildup.*
- ❑ *If a refrigerator was provided, it must be cleaned out, washed thoroughly and unplugged with the door left open.*
- ❑ *Do not leave any appliances belonging to the tenant such as a washer/dryer without the prior permission of the owner.*
- ❑ *All cupboards must be cleaned on the inside and any shelf paper removed.*
- ❑ *All windows must be washed inside and out.*
- ❑ *Any mini-blinds must be cleaned.*
- ❑ *All nails and hooks must be carefully removed from the walls. (Do not patch holes)*
- ❑ *All of the baseboards must be wiped down.*
- ❑ *All light fixtures are expected to have working light bulbs installed.*
- ❑ *The fireplace is to be cleaned of any ashes.*
- ❑ *Any fireplace tools or screen provided for your use are to remain with the rental.*
- ❑ *The lawns must be mowed and the planters must be weed free.*

- *The yard must be free of any trash or litter.*
- *Any pet feces must be picked up and disposed of in the trash. Do not throw cat litter in the yard.*
- *Any hoses or sprinklers provided with the rental are to remain with the rental.*
- *The garage must be swept out and any car grease or oil on the floor removed.*
- *Do not leave any chemicals, old paint etc. in the garage or under the sinks.*
- *The patio, front porch and any sidewalks are to be swept or hosed off.*
- *Leave any doormats provided with the rental.*
- *Do not remove any plants or trees that have been planted into the ground at this rental.*

If we have to pay to clean any potion of the rental or to remove any items left behind, these expenses will be deducted from your deposit amount. Also any damage that has been done to this rental will be assessed to your Security Deposit amount. If the Security Deposit amount is insufficient for these expenses, you will be billed for them. We will provide you with a written itemized accounting of any such expenses within two weeks (14 days) of our walk through inspection.

Please phone us at _____when you are ready for us to do a Walk Through Inspection after you are fully moved out and have cleaned the premises. If you desire a walk-though inspection before you move out, we can do that also to give you some idea of areas that might need repair or cleaning. Also please make sure that you have returned any keys and the automatic garage door opener (if applicable).

You will need to provide us with a forwarding address where we can send the remaining deposit.

Thank you for your attention to these details.

Owner_____

Date_____

It's my rental and I'll cry if I want to…

After the tenant moves out—you move in to survey the damage and to see what you will need to do to get your unit back in rentable condition once again. That first glimpse of the vacated rental is like opening door # 3 on "Let's Make a Deal." You never know if it will reveal a fabulous prize or a load of chicken manure. Sometimes you are delighted with the way the tenant has cleaned the rental…sometimes you just want to cry.

The worst-case scenario is when a tenant has left under duress, like after a forced eviction. He is behind in the rent and has long ago used up any security deposit he had plus some. This deadbeat tenant has no incentive to move, let alone to clean.

The Dysfunctional Tenant

Ms. Gallo was an alcoholic. When she first moved in, she held a responsible job and paid the rent. But as time went on she lost both her job and her way. By the time she moved out she was in the end stages of alcohol poisoning. I knew it was bad, but I was unprepared to see just how trashed the rental house actually was. Ms. Gallo left most of her possessions and some very bad impressions behind. The poor house looked as if the tenant had just walked out after a disastrous three-year binge. The sink and kitchen countertops were piled high with dirty dishes caked with dried-on food. The refrigerator was stacked with pots and containers of no longer identifiable rotting matter. The floor color was indecipherable under a thick layer of grime that stuck to your shoes. Grease ran down the sides of the stove which was covered in baked-on food and unwashed skillets. Each bedroom looked as if a bomb had gone off. Clothes and assorted junk littered the beds and floors. Closets hung open disgorging clothing and boxes of junk. Piles of shoes, old magazines, and broken appliances gathered dust along the edges of each room. Curtains hung in tatters. Every mini-blind was shredded. The bathroom was mildewed. The faucets dripped, rusting the sinks and floors. The sink and tub were black with grime, the shower curtain hung by a thread. And I won't even describe the toilet. As if all this was not bad enough, behind the kitchen door was the *pie'ce de re'sistance*—the decimated skeleton of a tiny bird. The idea that Mrs. Gallo had lived like this made me shudder.

Stanley, a single Dad, needed the three bedrooms with nice fenced back yard for himself and his two kids. We sorely misjudged his ability to pay the rent as well as the remarkable ability of his kids to demolish the place. By the time the eviction was complete, the back fence lay in broken pieces strewn across the lawn. The front brick retaining wall was missing the entire top cement cap, which had been hammered off a piece at a time and thrown on the sidewalk. The nice vertical blinds in the dining room were mostly ripped down and stomped in the mud outside. The closet doors were removed. The carpeting was a mass of spots, drips and spills. Several ceiling fan blades were missing, and every light fixture was missing or broken. Did I mention that Stanley also left a line of trash bags oozing along the front walk, and a stash of unpaid bills in the kitchen drawer? A renter can always move to fresh digs whenever his present nest is trashed.

Left Behind

It is after the move out that you find little surprises like the cigarette butts in the fireplace from the tenant who swore he was a non-smoker, or the dog poop and urine stained carpet in the bedrooms left by the dog he didn't have. One tenant who had a bug phobia had sealed all the windows shut with silicone. Another had re-keyed all of the door locks. Instead of using a lint bucket, one tenant whose washer/dryer was in the kitchen area had vented the dryer up into the attic space instead. You can imagine the fire danger of an attic full of lint.

By the time a tenant moves, he has usually accumulated a lot of junk that he no longer wants or needs; things like old worn out washers and dryers, derelict TV's, broken furniture, used tires, toxic paint, used motor oil, and empty pots. If he doesn't want it, you're stuck with it. Other large items left at our rentals have been several non-running cars and the front-end clip from a Camaro, weighing in at about 250 pounds. When large items are left behind, this kind of cleanup can be costly. In severe cases, a large dumpster must be rented to dispose of the mass of trash left behind.

The deadbeat tenant usually takes the good stuff with him and leaves the trash behind…literally. You can tell a challenging cleanup by the smell.

Ginger, the tenant of a small house finally moved out after many heated words and a long eviction process. She left a little present behind. On the front porch roasting in the summer sun rested ten huge plastic sacks of old rotting garbage. The bags were ripped at the bottom edge, releasing a fowl smelling, maggot infested ooze across the porch. At this rental we paid for trash service and an empty trashcan sat a few feet away…but this was payback. The rest of the house was not much better. I guess Ginger wasn't planning to include us on her next resume.

Landlording isn't for the faint of heart, stomach or muscle.

Who's Property is It?

One of the ironies of rental property is that tenants often leave behind things that they brought, and take things with them that you supplied for their use, but not for their possession. If it is not nailed down, or even if it is, many items you have bought for the rental make the move to greener pastures. Shower curtains, garden hoses, mirrors, fireplace tools, doormats, entire doors, the kitchen stove, and even light bulbs have been known to defect. One tenant dug up each and every plant around the house, leaving gaping holes behind. If only the departing tenant would be so kind as to take the kitchen grease and the mildew in the shower with him as well.

When I stepped in to water the browning lawn at a rental where a move out was in progress, I could not find either of the hoses or sprinklers we had provided. *"Oh yeah,"* mumbled the tenant, *"I told my ex-boyfriend he could have them."*

"Oh, yeah?" I responded, *"Then unless you want to pay to replace them plus the dying lawn, I suggest you have him bring them right back."* The hoses and sprinklers mysteriously returned.

Getting it Right

When a tenant gives you notice that he plans to move out, encourage him to leave the rental in good condition: a condition as close as possible to the condition it was in when he took possession. His motivation to do this is to get back his full security deposit. If you have a tenant in good standing who is the conscientious sort, he might do a great job of cleaning up. When a tenant makes a good honest effort to leave the rental nice, I try to refund the full security deposit amount. I want to be fair and I really do appreciate a rental left in good condition.

On the other hand, if you have a tenant who has already illegally run out most of his security deposit as a last month's rent (especially one involved in an eviction) you have very little leverage to encourage him to clean up the rental. If he doesn't pay the rent, he probably won't clean. He often will not bother to take all of his possessions, vacuum the carpet, or even flush the toilet. So plan on extra work and expense after this tenant. This is not a situation where you will want to show the rental before the move out.

This is the tenant after whose tenancy you very possibly might say, *"It's my rental and I'll cry if I want to."* You cry tears of relief in getting rid of a bad tenant, and tears of disbelief at the shambles to which your rental has been reduced.

What to Do—Before the Move-out

Your goal when taking back possession of the rental property is to get it cleaned up and back onto the market as soon as possible. Since the down time between tenants is a financial loss for you, if you can plan ahead, you can move things along faster.

You can plan ahead for this when first given the 30-day notice. First of all, give your vacating tenant the **Tenant Move-Out Checklist***. This tells him what you expect. I also ask the tenant if anything is broken or not working at the rental. This gives me a heads-up as to what repairs might be needed.

Before the tenant has actually moved out you can line up a painter, a carpet cleaner (if the tenant is not likely to do so), and buy some of the replacement parts or appliances you know you will need. Line up a locksmith to change the locks. You can also have the electricity transferred temporarily into your name when the tenant vacates so your workmen will have power.

The Tenant Move-Out Checklist

Fortunately many tenants are nice, decent folks who appreciate the housing you have provided. This tenant has taken good care of the rental and wants to leave it clean. For this tenant it can be helpful to provide a **Tenant Move-Out Checklist*** like the one shown at the beginning of this chapter. This way he will know exactly what you want done and what is expected of him by way of cleanup.

When I first began to compile this list, I was surprised at how long it grew. Yet I realized that each of these items, from having the carpets cleaned to mowing the lawn, were things that I would have to do or pay to have done if the tenant did not. So if the moving tenant follows the list he saves you a lot of work and guarantees himself (baring any damage) a full refund of his deposit. A tear out **Tenant Move-Out Checklist*** is provided in the back of this book.

It is also required by law that you inform your tenant at least 15 days prior to his move out that if he desires it, you will do a walk-through inspection prior to his move out. This might help him to be made aware of any areas that might be deducted from his security deposit. This walk-through could give him time to make some needed repair or do extra cleanup. You should use your original **Walk-through Inspection Form*** for this, noting what damage has occurred since the move-in. This walk-through is not your final one and does not preclude other deductions if more damage occurs or was hidden by furniture, rugs, etc. If this legal notification offer of inspection is not given, the tenant can sue to have his full security deposit refunded, regardless of the condition of the rental. This notification is included in the **Tenant Move-Out Checklist***.

Exclusive of ordinary wear and tear, the tenant is expected to leave the rental in the same condition in which he found it.

The most important item on this list is the removal of all of his personal property. As you will see in the next section, any abandoned property left behind by your tenant creates headaches for you.

Two other trouble spots are the carpeting and the cupboards:

Carpet Cleaning

It is important for the tenant to have the carpet "professionally" cleaned. Make it clear that you do not want the tenant to rent a carpet-cleaning machine to attempt to clean it himself. This can damage the carpeting by putting too much water into the padding or by frizzing up the top carpet fibers. A professional cleaning is also needed to permanently remove most spots.

Cupboards/Cabinets

Another area I encourage the departing tenant to tackle is pulling up the old shelf paper from the cupboards. This can be a time consuming job if the paper is stuck, yet a necessary step for a neat and clean rental. The cupboards should also be wiped out on the inside and wiped down on the outside, especially in the kitchen.

A nice inexpensive upgrade for a kitchen or bath is to replace the cabinet knobs or handles. Following a paint job or cleaning, putting on new knobs makes the cabinets look new again.

The Yuck Factor

Brace yourself for the yuck factor. Sometimes you will have some dirty work to do. So clothespin your nose and try not to take a deep breath.

One of the worst cleanup items for you as a landlord is a refrigerator that has been unplugged and left standing with old food still inside. The putrid water running out from the defrosting freezer portion, which is ruining the vinyl flooring, is only the start of your troubles. Next you have to hold your nose while cleaning out someone else's old food spills and rotting produce. (Remember that I recommend against providing a refrigerator) Even a refrigerator that has been cleaned out and washed by the tenant can be a real mildewy mess if the door has then been shut.

A tenant in a hurry will take their refrigerator and leave the mess under it for you to clean up.

Bathrooms can also be left in deplorable condition. Find a good cleanser that removes calcium build up from toilets and showers, and get a heavy-duty pair of gloves. Better yet, if you can afford it, find a good cleaning agency.

The cleanup I dread the most is a pet mess, especially one from an unauthorized pet. It is no picnic having to pull up carpeting rank with urine or even to clean up a yard where doggie doo doo has been allowed to accumulate.

And the term "landlord" sounds so glamorous…

Abandoned Property

After the tenant is gone, you need to restore the rental to good condition as soon as possible. Time is money. There are several steps to this process. The first step is to remove any trash or tenant personal property left behind.

When a tenant leaves property behind, you have to determine how to deal with it. Is it trash or something the tenant might want to have back? The sack of rotting food you can safely throw away, but what about that box of old clothes?

Because personal property belongs to the tenant—not to you—there are laws you must follow in dealing with anything left behind.

If the personal property is believed by you to be worth less that $300, you must do the following: You must give the tenant a written notice of his right to reclaim the abandoned personal property. A **Notice of Right to Reclaim Abandoned Personal Property*** form is located in the back of this book. On this form you must give a reasonable description of the items left behind and list where the items are being stored. If an item has just been left outside on the lawn, you can legally leave it there. However, this is not attractive for renting to your future prospective tenants. If an item was left inside the house or garage, you must provide a secure storage for it. You must store this property in a secure location (such as a storage facility or in the locked garage) for 18 days after the notice was deposited in the mail. If the tenant fails to reclaim his property during this time limit, you may keep, sell or destroy these items without further notice to the tenant.

Tenants do come back for their property, although not usually all of it, especially not the trash. The tenant can be asked to pay for the reasonable cost of storage for these items if you have paid for a storage facility or even if you have stored the items in the garage of the rental. The tenant is unlikely to pay up, however, and you cannot withhold property as payment.

If the tenant leaves property that has a value greater than $300, things get more complicated. You must give the same notice and offer the same right to claim the property within 18 days.

However, because this property has more value, if it is not reclaimed within the 18-day period you cannot just dispose of it, sell it, or keep it. It must be sold at a public sale, which has been duly advertised in a publication such as a newspaper. The tenant can bid on his property at this sale. You, as the landlord, can deduct your costs for storage, advertising and the sale, but then the remaining money from this sale must be paid over to the county to be held in a special fund. The tenant can claim the remaining money at any time within one year after the county receives these funds. As you can see, this is a time consuming and involved process. So hope that your tenant doesn't leave too many real treasures behind.

Toxic Leftovers

You may need to have an extra trash pickup or have a trash dumpster delivered if there is a lot of trash left at a rental. Sometimes, if there are a lot of large junk items, it pays to have a hauling company take the mess away. All of these expenses can be deducted from the security deposit.

Often a tenant will leave toxic or hazardous substances behind. These are such things as household cleaners, old paint, used motor oil, paint thinners, gasoline, and even used tires. You must be careful to dispose of these items in a safe and legal manner. You cannot just throw toxic substances in the trash. Hazardous waste centers will take many of these items. Tire centers will take old tires for a small fee.

Because these items are troublesome for your tenant to discard legally, you'll often be stuck with some toxic leftovers to dispose of. Don't panic, but don't be complacent about leaving them for the next tenant to deal with either.

Wear and Tear

After all the possessions have been cleared out, the second step is to assess what needs to be repaired, replaced, cleaned or painted before renting the unit again. The **Tenant Move Out Checklist*** and the **Walk-through Inspection Form*** are two forms that will help you determine what is damaged and what else need to be done.

Damaged items need to be assessed quickly as you need to charge the replacement or repair of such items against the security deposit amount within a 14-day period. This means that you will have to have the item replaced or repaired quickly to have a bill to submit to your former tenant. This bill will substantiate any repair or replacement costs deducted from his security deposit.

Some things in a house just wear out. Carpeting, faucets, and appliances all need to be replaced from time to time. You cannot charge a tenant for a bit of wear on the carpeting. You can charge him for damage to new carpeting or stains that won't come out.

A helpful guide in determining what constitutes wear and tear is this schedule of expected replacement:

Fixtures and Appliances—10 years

Paint—3 years

Draperies and blinds—7 years

Carpeting—4 years

If an item is nearing the end of its useful life, the space between tenants is a good time to replace it. This way a tenant living in the rental is not inconvenienced and you have a nice upgrade as an inducement for the next tenant. This is also a good time to make any improvements you've been contemplating. If you're ready to put in a new stove, re-roof the house, replace the old tile countertop, put in new carpeting, or new vinyl flooring in the kitchen—now is the time.

What to do—After the Move-out

I like to check the rental right after the tenant has moved out. This gives me an idea of the condition of the rental and the job ahead. I use the **Walk Through Inspection Form*** that was filled out with the tenant before he moved in. On this form I make note of any damage. Then I arrange to do a second walk through with the tenant using the same form.

At this time I can point out any damage or thank the tenant for leaving the rental in great shape. If the tenant has just left with no forwarding address and is not around for a walk through, I detail any damage in a letter when I refund any security deposit left. If the rental has been left in good shape, I express my thanks in a letter as well. This makes a good reference for the tenant to take with him.

If any abandoned property has been left I promptly move it into the garage or storage if necessary and get that letter out. I want those 18 days of storage to be over long before I need to show the unit to a prospective tenant. Otherwise the last tenant's junk can get in the way of renting the unit.

No matter how good your last tenant was, some routine maintenance is a given. I usually repaint the interior walls, cupboards, etc. between each tenant unless it has been a very short tenancy. There will be nail holes in the walls and fade marks behind the missing pictures not to mention some dirt and grime. I ask the tenant to remove any nails in the wall but not to patch the holes. This is because a poor patching job can create more problems than it solves. If a patching material is put on too thickly or not wiped off in time, it takes a lot of sanding to restore the wall.

A coat of paint really freshens up the look of a house or apartment. Find a good painter with reasonable rates. You'll be seeing a lot of him.

Go over your **Walk Through Inspection Form*** and attend to any problem areas that you noted. Decide if the item should be repaired, replaced, cleaned or simply removed. Line up workmen to do any of the jobs you don't want to tackle yourself. Try not to let the repairs drag out too long.

Decide which areas need some serious work like a new carpet or new vinyl flooring or a new tub surround in the bathroom. Make these areas a priority and get the needed workmen lined up as soon as possible.

Always check the electrical receptacles and wall plates as these can become damaged or go missing. Replace any damaged receptacles and make sure each set of wall plugs and light switches has a plate. Safety first.

Also check that the heating/air-conditioning are working and also the yard sprinkling systems.

What work will the yard need? You will need to water it to keep the plants alive between tenants and probably mow as well.

And finally…you are down to clean up. You can use the **Tenant Move Out Checklist*** for an overview which areas still need cleaning. Did the tenant wash out the cupboards and remove the shelf paper? Did he thoroughly clean the bathroom? Did the windows get washed? Will you do the cleaning or will you hire someone else to do it? Note: it is easier to bill a tenant for cleaning expenses when you have paid someone to clean rather than when you have done it yourself, as there is no proof of the hours you actually put in or your going rate.

A Picture is Worth a Thousand Excuses

If the move-out involves an eviction or damage, your camera is your friend. I always take photos of any real damage to verify it if needed in court. I also take photos of any portions of the rental that are left in a trashed condition. This way if the tenant questions the need for extensive cleanup or trash removal, I have the destruction recorded on film. Also take photos of any abandoned property left behind. Was that table a valuable heirloom or a dinged up cheap castoff? Was that TV a wide screen or a screen with a bullet hole in the dead center that was being used as a flowerpot? Your photo will tell the tale. Photos also authenticate how much stuff was left behind that needed to be stored, thus validating storage expenses. Photos can be stored on your computer or on a CD for easy retrieval. If you really want to be thorough, you can also protect yourself by taking "before" photos of the condition of the rental between tenants.

Damage

A little wear and tear is to be expected. Damage is something else. I really don't expect the average tenant to break a window, punch holes in the walls, crack the tile on the countertops, or break a light fixture in the rental. These types of destruction are beyond the normal realm of wear and tear and constitute rental damage. Repairing or replacing appliances or fixtures, replacing broken windows or walls are expenses that can be deducted from the security deposit amount. These expenses can be charged to a tenant who doesn't have a large enough deposit amount left over to cover these expenses. Good luck collecting, however.

Refund the Security Deposit

Once the damage (if any) has been repaired, and any cleaning done, you can deduct these amounts from the Security Deposit. You should also deduct any rent that is owed. The Security Deposit is discussed in detail in Chapter 14. Then refund the remainder to your tenant using the **Disposition of Security Deposit*** form within the 14-day period after the tenant has vacated the rental. If your tenant was a good one, take this opportunity to include your written "thank you" note in the same envelope.

Don't Take it Personally

Surveying a rental that has been abused is an emotional event—one where the "after" snapshot is a sorry degradation of the mint condition of the "before" photo in your memory or in your file.

When the nest (a nest you own) is fouled, it tends to hurt. After a particularly bad move out, as I am surveying a really awful mess…again, I tend to freak out a bit. I think of how lovely the house was when the tenant moved in. I look at the filthy, stained carpet that was brand new just six months ago. I look at the mini-blinds, which are listing askew with broken stings and missing panels. I look at the huge gashes on the vinyl flooring left behind from moving out the fridge. I try not to look at the cracked sink, the broken window, and the trashed yard.

At this moment, my husband reminds me. *"It's only money, Honey."* I own this home but it is not **my** home. With a little money and some elbow grease it can be set right again. I don't have to take it personally. This is just part of the rental business. The part I don't like so much. But it is not cancer. It is not a failed marriage or a ruined business. It is just the leavings of a thoughtless or maybe dysfunctional tenant. If I can remember this and keep a bit of detachment, I can tackle starting over once again.

Starting Over

After you have removed all the tenant belongings, have repaired or replaced any broken items, have cleaned, have had the walls painted and the carpets cleaned, and have made any needed improvements, you've come full circle. You are ready to find a new tenant for your rental. An empty refurbished rental is like a new house. It smells of fresh paint, and new carpeting, with a trace of pine cleaner. It has all the hope and promise of a new beginning. You've put a lot of time effort and money into restoring it to move-in condition. So take your time. Find the perfect tenant for this home.

Clean up/Starting Over Checklist

Before the Tenant Leaves

- ❏ Give the tenant the **Tenant Move-Out Checklist***.
- ❏ Ask if anything needs replacement or repair.
- ❏ Line up any workmen you will need.
- ❏ Arrange for electricity in be put in your name if needed.

After the Tenant Moves Out

- ❏ Do a walk through with your **Walk Through Inspection Sheet***.
- ❏ Note what repairs are needed.
- ❏ If possible, arrange a walk through with your tenant.
- ❏ Take photos of any damage, extensive trash, or abandoned property.
- ❏ Give written notice to the tenant re. any abandoned property.
- ❏ Store abandoned property.
- ❏ Haul away any trash.

- ❑ Properly dispose of any hazardous waste.
- ❑ Do any needed repairs or improvements.
- ❑ Do routine maintenance like painting or cleaning.
- ❑ Legally dispose of any abandoned property not claimed.
- ❑ Refund the Security Deposit less any money used for damages or cleaning.
- ❑ Write a "thank you" note to your good tenant.
- ❑ Remember not to take it personally when a rental is damaged.
- ❑ Start over with your search for the next tenant.

You are the Landlord…always believe—the perfect tenant is out there somewhere.

This form is found at the back of this book.

Summary

So you want to be a landlord? Good for you. Even if there are a lot of potential problems in rental management, you can head off most of them by doing your homework and background research such as reading this book and other relevant literature.

Using this book, you can flip to the applicable section or even just the Checklist as a reminder of what to keep in mind in various issues with tenants. All of these areas don't hit all at once, and can be easily managed one at a time. Be sure to consult an attorney for the most current advice about any legal issues.

As a landlord, you will learn a lot about people and about yourself. You may even learn a few virtues like patience and forgiveness.

When looking at the current alternatives to investing your money, real estate, to me, is still the best game in town. Would I do it again? In a heartbeat.

Happy investing. Your life will never be boring again.

Appendix: Rental Forms

Rental Forms List

- ❏ Rental Application
- ❏ Rental Agreement Month-to-Month
- ❏ Rental Agreement Yearly Lease
- ❏ Addendum
- ❏ Walk Through Inspection Checklist
- ❏ Tenant Move Out Checklist
- ❏ 30-Day Notice
- ❏ 60-Day Notice
- ❏ 3-Day Pay or Quit Notice
- ❏ 24-Hour Right of Entry Notice
- ❏ Notice of Rent Increase
- ❏ Notice of right to Reclaim Abandoned Personal Property
- ❏ Disposition of Security Deposit
- ❏ Lead Based Paint Warning Statement

Rental Application
Each proposed adult tenant must full out a separate application

Name _____ Social Security #_____

Home Phone _____

Birth Date (Month, Day, Year)_____/_____/_____ Driver's License Number_____

Address	Street	City	Zip	From	To	Owner	Phone #
Present							
Previous							
Next Previous							

How Many in your family? Adults_____ Children_____

Proposed Occupants	Relationship	Age of minor children

Occupation:	Present Occupation	Previous Occupation
Employer		
Business Address		
Business Phone		
Name of Supervisor		
From:	To:	From: To:
Monthly Salary		

Financial Obligations:

Payments to:	Address	Monthly Payment $
Payments to:	Address	Monthly Payment $
Payments to:	Address	Monthly Payment $

Personal References:	Address	Phone	Occupation
1.			
2.			
3.			

Credit Check Authorization

Do you authorize and agree to pay for a credit check? Yes_____ No_____

Information

Do you smoke? Yes_____ No_____

Do you have any pets? If so describe_____

Have you ever been evicted? Yes_____ No_____
      If Yes, please explain on a separate sheet of paper

Terms of the Agreement

The undersigned is making application for the apartment or house located at

_____City_____ CA.

The applying tenant understands that the rent for this unit is $_____per month payable in advance on the first of every month.

The applying tenant also understands that a security deposit in the amount of $_____is required prior to move in. This deposit can be used by the landlord if necessary for non payment of rent, cleaning or repairs. It is not to be used as a last month's rent.

Tenant Applicant_____
Date_____20____.
        Signature

Rental Agreement
Month-to-Month

This agreement has been entered into on the _____ day of _____

20_____. It is by and between _____ Owner (Landlord)

and _____ Tenant (Resident)

In consideration of their mutual promises, the parties agree as follows:

Section 1

The Owner rents to the Tenant and the Tenant rents from the Owner for residential use only the premises known as:

_____, _____ _____.
                           Street Address   State   Zip Code

Section 2

Rent is due in advance on the 1st day of each and every month at the rate of $_____ per month, beginning on the _____ day of _____ 20____. A five percent late fee will be assessed for any late rent payments. See Addendum.

Section 3

This agreement may be terminated by either party after service upon the other of a written 30-day notice of termination of tenancy. Any holding over thereafter will result in the tenant being liable to the owner for **rental damages** at the fair rental value of $_____ per day.

Section 4

The premises shall be occupied only by the following named person(s):
(Include birth date if under 18.)

_____   _____
Name   Birth date   Name   Birth date

_____   _____
Name   Birth date   Name   Birth date

Section 5

No portion of the said premises shall be sublet nor this agreement assigned. The Tenant is prohibited from renting out rooms, taking in an unapproved roommate or long-term guest, or from giving over his lease to another party. Any attempted subletting or assignment by the Tenant shall, at the election of the Owner, be an irremediable breach of this agreement.

Section 6

The stay of any guest is to be very short-term. No more than 3 days per year. See Addendum.

Section 7

The Tenant shall pay for all utilities, services and charges except:

_____.

Section 8

Pets

❑ No pets are allowed at this rental.

❑ The only pets approved at this rental are_____

_____.

A Pet Deposit in the amount of $_____was paid on_____.
See Addendum for details of pet management.

Section 9

The Tenant shall not violate any governmental law in the use of these premises. He shall not commit waste or nuisance. Nor shall he annoy, molest or interfere with any other resident or neighbor.

Section 10

The Tenant shall make no repairs, decorating improvements, or alterations without the Owner's prior written or verbal consent. The Tenant shall notify the Owner in writing of any repairs or alterations contemplated and receive approval before the changes are made. See Addendum.

Section 11

The Owner is **not** financially responsible for any improvements made without his consent or agreement to cover the cost. Therefore, the Tenant shall hold the Owner harmless as to any mechanics lien recordation or proceeding caused by the Tenant.

Section 12

The Tenant shall keep the premises and fixtures, furnishings and appliances, plumbing, yard and landscaping, which are rented for the Tenant's exclusive use in good working order and condition. See Addendum.

Section 13

The Tenant shall pay the Owner for the costs to repair, replace or rebuild any portion of the premises damaged by the Tenant, the Tenant's guests or invitees.

Section 14

The Tenant's personal property is not insured by the Owner.

Section 15

Security Deposit

The Tenant shall deposit with the Owner, as a **Security Deposit**, the sum of $_____ payable _____20_____.

The Security Deposit amount is **not** a last month's rent and may not be used as such by the Tenant. The Owner may claim and withhold from the Security Deposit only such amounts as are reasonably necessary to remedy tenant defaults as follows:

a. for payment of rent, or

b. to repair damages to the premises caused by the Tenant, exclusive of ordinary wear and tear, or

c. to clean such premises, if necessary, upon termination of the tenancy.

No later than two weeks (14 days) after the Tenant has vacated the premises, the Owner shall furnish the Tenant with an itemized written statement of the basis for, and the amount of, any Security Deposit received and the disposition of this deposit and shall return any remaining portion of this deposit to the Tenant.

For this purpose, the Tenant is requested to leave with the Owner a forwarding address when vacating this rental.

Section 16

If any legal action or proceeding is brought by either party to enforce any part of this rental agreement, the prevailing party shall recover any reasonable attorney's fees and costs, in addition to all other relief.

Section 17

Notice upon the Owner may be served upon:_____

at _____.

Section 18

The premises are equipped with at least one and possibly more smoke detectors. It is the Tenant's responsibility to see that the smoke detector(s) battery is replaced as needed to keep the smoke detector in operating condition at all times.

Section 19

The Tenant has inspected the premises, and fixtures and appliances and has found them to be operative and satisfactory.

Section 20

The undersigned Tenant(s) whether or not in actual possession of the premises are jointly and severally liable for all obligations under this rental agreement and for any property damage done by any Tenant, their guest, and invitees.

Section 21

The Tenant also agrees to the terms of the attached rental **Addendum.**

The undersigned Tenant(s) acknowledge having read, understood and agreed to the foregoing terms. The Tenant has received a duplicate of the original.

_____   _____
Tenant   Date   Owner   Date

_____   _____
Tenant   Date

Rental Agreement
Yearly Lease

This agreement has been entered into on the _____day of _____

20_____. It is by and between _____Owner (Landlord)

and _____Tenant (Resident)

In consideration of their mutual promises, the parties agree as follows:

Section 1

The Owner rents to the Tenant and the Tenant rents from the Owner for residential use only the premises known as:

_____, _____ _____.
Street Address   State Zip   Code

Section 2

Rent is due in advance on the 1st day of each and every month at the rate of $_____per month, beginning on the _____day of _____20____. A five percent late fee will be assessed for any late rent payments. See Addendum.

Section 3

This agreement may be terminated by either party (after the year lease period) after service upon the other of a written 30-day notice of termination of tenancy. Any holding over thereafter will result in the tenant being liable to the owner for **rental damages** at the fair rental value of $_____per day.

Section 4

The premises shall be occupied only by the following named person(s):
(Include birth date if under 18.)

_____	_____	_____	_____
Name	Birth date	Name	Birth date
_____	_____	_____	_____
Name	Birth date	Name	Birth date

Section 5

No portion of the said premises shall be sublet nor this agreement assigned. The Tenant is prohibited from renting out rooms, taking in an unapproved roommate or long-term guest, or from giving over his lease to another party. Any attempted subletting or assignment by the Tenant shall, at the election of the Owner, be an irremediable breach of this agreement.

Section 6

The stay of any guest is to be very short-term. No more than 3 days per year. See Addendum.

Section 7

The Tenant shall pay for all utilities, services and charges except:

_____.

Section 8

Pets

❑ No pets are allowed at this rental.

❑ The only pets approved at this rental are_____

_____.

A Pet Deposit in the amount of $_____was paid on_____.
See Addendum for details of pet management.

Section 9

The Tenant shall not violate any governmental law in the use of these premises. He shall not commit waste or nuisance. Nor shall he annoy, molest or interfere with any other resident or neighbor.

Section 10

The Tenant shall make no repairs, decorating improvements, or alterations without the Owner's prior written or verbal consent. The Tenant shall notify the Owner in writing of any repairs or alterations contemplated and receive approval before the changes are made. See Addendum.

Section 11

The Owner is **not** financially responsible for any improvements made without his consent or agreement to cover the cost. Therefore, the Tenant shall hold the Owner harmless as to any mechanics lien recordation or proceeding caused by the Tenant.

Section 12

The Tenant shall keep the premises and fixtures, furnishings and appliances, plumbing, yard and landscaping, which are rented for the Tenant's exclusive use in good working order and condition. See Addendum.

Section 13

The Tenant shall pay the Owner for the costs to repair, replace or rebuild any portion of the premises damaged by the Tenant, the Tenant's guests or invitees.

Section 14

The Tenant's personal property is not insured by the Owner.

Section 15

Security Deposit

The Tenant shall deposit with the Owner, as a **Security Deposit**, the sum of $_____ payable _____20_____.

The Security Deposit amount is **not** a last month's rent and may not be used as such by the Tenant. The Owner may claim and withhold from the Security Deposit only such amounts as are reasonably necessary to remedy tenant defaults as follows:

a. for payment of rent, or

b. to repair damages to the premises caused by the Tenant, exclusive of ordinary wear and tear, or

c. to clean such premises, if necessary, upon termination of the tenancy.

No later than two weeks (14 days) after the Tenant has vacated the premises, the Owner shall furnish the Tenant with an itemized written statement of the basis for, and the amount of, any Security Deposit received and the disposition of this deposit and shall return any remaining portion of this deposit to the Tenant.

For this purpose, the Tenant is requested to leave with the Owner a forwarding address when vacating this rental.

Section 16

If any legal action or proceeding is brought by either party to enforce any part of this rental agreement, the prevailing party shall recover any reasonable attorney's fees and costs, in addition to all other relief.

Section 17

Notice upon the Owner may be served upon:_____

at _____.

Section 18

The premises are equipped with at least one and possibly more smoke detectors. It is the Tenant's responsibility to see that the smoke detector(s) battery is replaced as needed to keep the smoke detector in operating condition at all times.

Section 19

The Tenant has inspected the premises, and fixtures and appliances and has found them to be operative and satisfactory.

Section 20

The undersigned Tenant(s) whether or not in actual possession of the premises are jointly and severally liable for all obligations under this rental agreement and for any property damage done by any Tenant, their guest, and invitees.

Section 21

The Tenant also agrees to the terms of the attached rental **Addendum.**

The undersigned Tenant(s) acknowledge having read, understood and agreed to the foregoing terms. The Tenant has received a duplicate of the original.

_____   _____
Tenant   Date   Owner   Date

_____   _____
Tenant   Date

Addendum
to Rental Agreement

Item 1—The Late Fee

Rent is due on the 1st of each month. It is important that the Owner receive the rent on time each month in order to pay the bills on the rental. The Owner extends to the Tenant a five-day grace period in paying the rent. Any rent not received by the 5th of each month will be considered late and will be subject to an automatic 5 percent late fee. This fee would be due and payable with the late rent. For example, the late fee on a $1000 monthly rent would be $50 for a total late rent due of $1050.

The purpose of this late fee is <u>not</u> to allow for late payment of rent, but to encourage the tenant to pay the rent on time. Continued late payment of the rent will be grounds for eviction.

Item 2—No Subletting

No portion of said premises shall be sublet nor this agreement assigned. This means that the Tenant may not rent out any room or portion of this rental at any time, nor can the tenant turn his lease over to any other party. Any attempted subletting or assignment by the Tenant shall, at the election of the Owner, be an irremediable breach of this agreement.

If the Tenant wishes to have another person not listed in his rental agreement live at any time in this rental property, the Owner must first approve it and the new Tenant must sign a lease agreement. Moving any person not listed in this rental agreement into the rental without approval will be considered a serious breach of this agreement.

Item 3—Guests.

Anyone not listed as an occupant in this rental agreement who spends time at this rental or who spends the night there is considered a guest. **The maximum stay for any guest is to be three days per year.** Anyone staying longer than this may do so only with the express permission of the Owner. This permission should be asked for well in advance of the visit and should be limited to rare occasions.

Item 4—Repairs and Alterations

The Tenant shall <u>not</u> make any repairs, decorating improvement, or alterations without the Owner's prior written or verbal consent.

Alteration include, but are not limited to: painting, wallpapering, hanging of posters or pictures (a limited number of pictures, 1-3 per wall, may be hung with small nails on the walls providing all the nails are removed before vacating); installing shelves, cabinets, or hooks that attach to the wall; replacing or removing fixtures, lights, mirrors, curtains, mini-blinds, carpeting, or window coverings; removing or planting any shrubbery or trees on the property.

Item 5—Trash

Trashcans are provided for the use of the Tenant. Your trash day is_____.

The Tenant should take his trash cans out to the curb each week prior to trash pickup time and move them promptly back behind the gate or wherever appropriately stored as soon as possible after the trash had been picked up. The Tenant is not to leave the trashcans out at the curb.

The **green** trashcan is for general trash. It is picked up each week. The other two cans are for **recycling** and are picked up on alternating weeks by a separate truck than the regular trash truck.

The **blue** trashcan is for recyclables like newspaper, glass, metal cans, and plastics. Newspapers should be bundled and tied, or placed in a paper or plastic sack at the top of the recycle can. Bottles should be rinsed out. Cardboard boxes need to be disassembled and folded flat. If they do not fit into the blue can, they can be tied with string and placed next to the blue can on its pick-up day.

The **brown** trashcan is for green-waste recycling. This means that any lawn trimmings, leaves, and plant material should be placed in this can. This material will be mulched, so do not put in anything that is not a pure plant material. Do not put these plant trimmings in plastic bags.

The Tenant is not to let any trash build up in the house or on this property. If the Tenant needs additional help in disposing of trash, please let the Owner know.

Item 6—Pets

Only the pets listed in your Rental Agreement may be kept at any time on this property. Any additional pets may be kept on this property only with the express written permission of the Owner.

An outside pet is expected to remain outside of the house at all times with the exception of the garage area.

The Tenant is expected to clean up any feces from this pet on a regular basis and not allow any odor to build up on the property. Any pet is to be kept reasonably quiet so as not to become a nuisance to the neighbors. Any pests such as fleas associated with the pet's presence on the property should be treated at the Tenant's expense.

Any damage done to the house, carpeting, fencing, or yard by this pet is the responsibility of the Tenant. Repair expenses will be deducted from the Security Deposit and/or the Pet Deposit. Repairs exceeding these amounts will be charged to the Tenant.

Item 7—Vehicles

Vehicles approved at this time on the property are:

Make	Year
Make	Year
Make	Year

The Owner desires to keep this rental property free from any unused, abandoned, or extra vehicles. This includes cars, trucks, boats, trailers, motor homes, campers, motorcycles, buses, etc. To this end, the Owner asks the Tenant to keep only the approved vehicles listed above on this rental property or on the street in front of or adjacent to this property at any time. No one is to live at any time in a vehicle or trailer on this property.

Any vehicle that drips oil or other fluids must be fixed or parked over a pan to prevent oil damage to the driveway or garage floor. Dispose of any used motor oil promptly and properly at an oil-recycling center.

Item 8—Rental Use

This rental is intended for residential use only. The Tenant may **not** use this rental property at any time to conduct any type of commercial business. This includes, but is not limited to: babysitting, child-care, car repairs, lessons, bookkeeping, consignment projects, massage, or any business which requires customers to come onto the property. The Owner's liability insurance does not cover such ventures. Any use of this property for such a business would be considered a breach of the Rental Agreement.

Item 9—Yard Maintenance

Your rental fees ☐ **do** ☐ **do not** include the service of a gardener.

The Owner expects the Tenant to assume responsibility for watering the lawn, trees, and plants and keeping them in good condition. The yard should be kept reasonably weed free. If a gardener is provided he will mow and edge the lawns and do any needed pruning. If no gardening services are provided, the Tenant is expected to mow and edge the lawn every 1-2 weeks.

No tree or plant is to be removed without the Owner's permission. Any plants put into the ground on this property become the property of the Owner and are not to be removed when the Tenant leaves. If the Tenant wishes to retain ownership of a tree or plant, he should plant it in a pot.

No severe pruning of trees or plants is allowed without the express permission of the Owner. The Tenant may maintain a small garden if space is available without removing any of the existing landscaping and with the permission of the Owner.

If the Owner is paying the water bill, it is expected that the Tenant will help by conserving water and not over-watering. If the Tenant's water bills become too high due to a garden, the situation would have to be reassessed to either discontinue the garden or have the Tenant pay any portion of the water bill over a reasonable base amount to be determined by the Owner.

Item 10—Plumbing

The Tenant shall keep the plumbing in good working order by not flushing items that will clog or impair the lines or septic system. Items that should not be put down the toilet are feminine hygiene products, diapers or condoms. Avoid putting watermelon rinds, eggshells, coffee grounds or large items down the garbage disposal.

The Tenant should report any leaking faucets, running toilets, or line stoppages or back up to the Owner immediately.

Item 11—Carport

The following applies if the rental is an apartment with a carport instead of a garage:

The carport should be used to store one vehicle and anything that will fit into the storage cabinet. The Tenant may provide his own lock for the storage cabinet. Nothing else (with the exception of a bicycle) should be stored in the carport. The Owner wishes to keep the carport area neat and clean and to prevent attracting stray cats or rodents. To this end, at no time is the tenant to store boxes, mattresses, tools, appliances, furniture or other items in the carport. Anything not fitting into the storage locker must be disposed of or stored elsewhere. This rule will be strictly enforced by the Owner.

Item 12—Apartment Landings

The following applies if the rental is an apartment with shared landings:

The upper landing of each apartment needs to be kept clear for easy tenant access to the surrounding apartments and for fire safety. For this reason, no furniture, tables, chairs, potted plants, Bar-B-Ques, wind chimes, tools, brooms, flags, bikes, hanging decorations or other objects can be allowed on the landings, or hanging from the roof beams. Small doormats on the floor are OK.

Item 13—Laundry Room

The following applies if the rental is an apartment with a shared laundry room:

The laundry room is for Tenant use only. Visitors may **not** use the laundry facilities at any time. Please follow the laundry room rules to keep the machines in good working order. Remove clothes promptly from the washer or dryer when done and wipe out the machines and clean the lint filter after each load.

The undersigned Tenant(s) acknowledges and agrees to abide by the terms of this Addendum to the Rental Agreement.

Tenant   Date

_____   _____

_____

Walk-Through Inspection Checklist

Move in Date: _____

Move Out Date: _____

Tenant Name: _____

Rental Address: _____

	Condition upon Move In	Condition upon Move Out
Kitchen		
Floor		
Walls/Ceiling		
Stove/Oven		
Refrigerator		
Sink		
Faucets		
Garbage Disposal		
Cabinets		
Countertop		
Light Fixtures		
Ceiling Fan		
Windows/Screens		
Window covering		
Other		
Living Room		
Carpeting		
Walls/Ceiling		
Light Fixtures		
Ceiling Fan		
Windows/Screens		
Window covering		
Fireplace		
Other		
Heating/Cooling		
Heater		
Air Conditioner		

	Condition upon Move In	Condition Upon Move Out
Den		
Carpeting		
Walls/Ceiling		
Light Fixtures		
Ceiling Fan		
Windows/Screens		
Window Covering		
Fireplace		
Door		
Bedroom 1		
Carpeting/Flooring		
Walls/Ceiling		
Light Fixtures		
Ceiling Fan		
Windows/Screens		
Window Covering		
Door		
Closet		
Other		
Bedroom 2		
Carpeting/Flooring		
Walls/Ceiling		
Light Fixtures		
Ceiling Fan		
Windows/Screens		
Window Covering		
Door		
Closet		
Other		
Bedroom 3		
Carpeting/Flooring		
Walls/Ceiling		
Light Fixtures		
Ceiling Fan		
Windows/Screens		
Window Covering		
Door		
Closet		

	Condition upon Move In	Condition upon Move Out

Bath 1

Flooring		
Walls/Ceiling		
Light Fixtures		
Exhaust Fan		
Heater		
Sink		
Bathtub/Shower		
Faucets		
Countertop		
Mirror		
Windows/Screens		
Window Covering		
Cabinets		
Medicine Cabinet		
Towel Racks		
Toilet		

Bath 2

Flooring		
Walls/Ceiling		
Light Fixtures		
Exhaust Fan		
Heater		
Sink		
Bathtub/Shower		
Faucets		
Countertop		
Mirror		
Windows/Screens		
Window Covering		
Cabinets		
Medicine Cabinet		
Towel Racks		
Toilet		

	Condition upon Move In	Condition upon Move Out
Dining Room		
Flooring		
Walls/Ceiling		
Light Fixtures		
Ceiling Fan		
Windows/Screens		
Window Covering		
Other		
Laundry Room		
Flooring		
Walls/Ceiling		
Cabinets		
Lights		
Garage		
Garage door		
Side door		
Automatic Opener		
Shelving		
Floor		
Cabinets		
Lights		
Other		
Yard		
Lawn		
Landscaping		
Sprinkling system		
Fence		
Patio		
Storage Shed		
# of hoses provided		
# of sprinklers provided		

Tenant Signature on Move In_____

Tenant Signature on Move Out_____

Tenant Move-Out Checklist

Tenant Name_____

Rental Address _____CA_____

Security Deposit Amount $_____ Received _____

As you are ending your tenancy with us we would like to inform you of what is expected by way of move out and cleaning in order to receive back your full Security Deposit refund. We expect to receive back possession of this rental in the same condition in which it was turned over for your use.

This means that the following jobs should be done:

- All tenant belongings must be removed from the house, garage and yard. This includes properly disposing of all trash, and removing **anything** brought onto the premises by the tenant. This includes items such as wind-chimes, bar-b-ques, furniture, appliances, old mattresses, tires, wood, Christmas lights, and empty pots.
- All closets and cupboards are to be totally emptied including the hangers.
- The carpeting must be professionally cleaned. (Do not attempt to clean it yourself with a rented machine, as this may damage the carpet.)
- Any vinyl or wood flooring must be clean and mopped. (Including where the refrigerator has been.)
- The stove and oven must be cleaned.
- Sinks and bathtubs must be scrubbed and free of mildew and soap scum.
- The toilets must be cleaned with no calcium buildup.
- If a refrigerator was provided, it must be cleaned out, washed thoroughly and unplugged with the door left open.
- Do not leave any appliances belonging to the tenant such as a washer/dryer without the prior permission of the owner.
- All cupboards must be cleaned on the inside and any shelf paper removed.
- All windows must be washed inside and out.
- Any mini-blinds must be cleaned.
- All nails and hooks must be carefully removed from the walls.
  (Do not patch holes.)
- All of the baseboards must be wiped down.
- All light fixtures are expected to have working light bulbs installed.
- The fireplace is to be cleaned of any ashes.
- Any fireplace tools or screen provided for your use are to remain with the rental.
- The lawns must be mowed and the planters must be weed free.
- The yard must be free of any trash or litter.
- Any pet feces must be picked up and disposed of in the trash. Do not throw cat litter in the yard.
- Any hoses or sprinklers provided with the rental are to remain with the rental.
- The garage must be swept out and any car grease or oil on the floor removed.
- Do not leave any chemicals, old paint etc. in the garage or under the sinks.

- The patio, front porch and any sidewalks are to be swept or hosed off.
- Leave any doormats provided with the rental.
- Do not remove any plants or trees that have been planted into the ground at this rental.

If we have to pay to clean any potion of the rental or to remove any items left behind, these expenses will be deducted from your deposit amount. Also any damage that has been done to this rental will be assessed to your Security Deposit amount. If the Security Deposit amount is insufficient for these expenses, you will be billed for them. We will provide you with a written itemized accounting of any such expenses within two weeks (14 days) of our walk through inspection.

Please phone us at _____ when you are ready for us to do a Walk-Through Inspection after you are fully moved out and have cleaned the premises. If you desire a walk-through inspection before you move out, we can do that also to give you some ideas of areas that might need repair or cleaning. Also please make sure that you have returned any keys and the automatic garage door opener (if applicable).

You will need to provide us with a forwarding address where we can send the remaining deposit.

Thank you for your attention to these details.

_____

Owner

Date_____

Thirty (30) Day Notice to Quit

TENANT(S)_____

PREMISES _____

Street Address

_____

| City | State | Zip Code |

TO TENANT(S) AND ALL PERSONS IN POSSESSION:

YOU ARE HEREBY NOTIFIED that the tenancy under which you occupy the premises shall end sixty (60) days after the date of service of a copy of this notice upon you, and you are required to quit and deliver up possession of the premises to the undersigned on or before that date.

IF YOU FAIL TO DO SO, legal proceedings will be instituted against you for possession of the premises, for forfeiture of the rental agreement, and for such monetary damages as may be allowed by law.

Dated this _____ day of _____, 20_____.

_____

Owner/Agent

Sixty (60) Day Notice to Quit

TENANT(S) _____

PREMISES _____
Street Address

_____

| City | State | Zip Code |

TO TENANT(S) AND ALL PERSONS IN POSSESSION:

YOU ARE HEREBY NOTIFIED that the tenancy under which you occupy the premises shall end sixty (60) days after the date of service of a copy of this notice upon you, and you are required to quit and deliver up possession of the premises to the undersigned on or before that date.

IF YOU FAIL TO DO SO, legal proceedings will be instituted against you for possession of the premises, for forfeiture of the rental agreement, and for such monetary damages as may be allowed by law.

Dated this _____ day of _____, 20_____.

_____
Owner/Agent

3-Day Pay Rent or Quit Notice

To:_____
Name

and any and all other occupants at:

_____
Address

WITHIN THREE (3) DAYS after the service on you of this notice, you are hereby required to pay to the undersigned Owner or his Agent, the rent owed for the premises listed above, of which you now have possession. The rent owing at this date is the sum of:

_____dollars. ($_____)

The rent owed is enumerated as follows:

$_____ Due From_____20_____ To_____20_____

$_____ Due From_____20_____ To_____20_____

$_____ Due From_____20_____ To_____20_____

OR QUIT AND DELIVER UP THE POSSESSON OF THE PREMISES.

YOU ARE FURTHER NOTIFIED that the Owner does hereby elect to declare the forfeiture of your lease or rental agreement under which you hold possession of the above-described premises. If you fail to perform or otherwise comply, the Qwner will institute legal proceedings to recover and take possession of said premises. This could result in a judgment against you including the costs for legal and attorney fees as well as any damages allowed by law for such unlawful detention.

_____   _____
Owner/Agent   Date

Twenty-Four (24) Hour Right of Entry
Notice

Date_____

Time_____

Name_____(and all other occupants)

Address _____

    Notice is hereby given that the Owner or Agent of this property will be entering to inspect the premises after twenty-four (24) hours have expired. Approximate time of this inspection will be: Date: _____
Time:_____

                                Signed:

                                _____

                                    Owner/Agent

Notification of Rent Increase

Date_____

To: _____(Tenant)

    This letter is to inform you of a rent increase for the rental located at_____.
Your rent which is currently $_____per month will increase to $_____per month beginning
on_____(date).

Rent is due on the 1st of each month.

    We try to keep our rents reasonable and below the market, which we are doing even with this increase. This rent
increase is necessary due to the steadily rising costs of your utilities (trash and water), rising interest rates, and increased
costs for insurance, maintenance, and property taxes.
    Thank you for your attention to this matter.

_____

Property Owner

Notice of Right to Reclaim
Abandoned Personal Property

To Tenant _____

Address_____

City_____ State_____ Zip Code _____

County_____

When vacated, the premises described above contained the following personal property:

Unless you pay the reasonable cost of storage for all the above described personal property and take possession of the property which you claim, not later than eighteen (18) days after this notice is deposited in the mail, this personal property may be disposed of pursuant to Civil code section 1988.

(Check the ONE box below which applies.)

❑ Because this property is believed to be worth less than $300, it may be kept, sold, or destroyed without further notice if you fail to reclaim it within the time limit indicated below.

❑ Because this property is believed to be worth more than $300, it will be sold if you fail to reclaim it. It will be sold at a public sale after notice has been given by publication. You have the right to bid on the property at this sale. After the property is sold and the cost of storage, advertising, and sale is deducted, the remaining money will be paid over to the county. You may claim the remaining money at any time within one (1) year after the county receives the money.

Date of mailing this notice:_____
Date of expiration of this notice:_____

You may claim this property at:_____
(Address where property may be claimed)

_____   _____
Owner Signature   Owner Address

Disposition of Security Deposits

Tenant(s) Names:_____

Rental Address_____

Move Out Date_____

Deposits

Security Deposit _____ $ _____

Pet Deposit _____ $ _____

Charges Against Deposit

Unpaid rent: From _____to_____ $ _____

Legal Fees: _____ $ _____

Cleaning: _____ $ _____

Utilities: _____ $ _____

Repairs: _____ $ _____

        _____ $ _____

        _____ $ _____

        _____ $ _____

        _____ $ _____

        _____ $ _____

        _____ $ _____

Miscellaneous: _____ $ _____

TOTAL CHARGES: $ _____

BALANCE DUE: _____TENANT _____ OWNER _____ $ _____

DATE PAID:_____ CHECK NUMBER _____

TENANT'S FORWARDING ADDRESS:_____

_____

OWNER'S SIGNATURE:_____

Addendum to Rental Agreement

Disclosure of Information on Lead-Based Paint and/or Lead-Base Paint Hazards

For rental housing located at:

_____   _____   _____   _____
Street Address   City   State   Zip Code

Lead Based Paint Warning Statement

Housing built before 1978 may contain lead-based paint. Lead from paint, paint chips, and dust can pose health hazards if not managed properly. Lead exposure is especially harmful to young children and pregnant women.

Landlord's Disclosure

_____The landlord has no knowledge of any lead-based paint or associated hazard in this housing.

_____ Known lead based paint or associated hazard is present in this housing.
        Explain:_____.

Renters Acknowledgment

_____The Landlord has informed the tenant that no known lead-based paint or associated hazard exists in this housing.
_____The Landlord has informed the tenant that a known lead-based paint or associated hazard exists in this housing.
        The landlord has given the tenant a pamphlet entitled, *Protect Your Family from Lead in Your Home.*

Certification of Accuracy

The following parties have reviewed the information above and certify, to the best of their knowledge, that the information they have provided is true and accurate.

_____   _____20_____
Landlord   Date

_____   _____20_____
Tenant   Date

0-595-31214-4

www.ingramcontent.com/pod-product-compliance
Lightning Source LLC
Chambersburg PA
CBHW081151180526
45170CB00006B/2029